The READY RESOURCE

for
RELIEF SOCIETY

TEACHINGS OF PRESIDENTS
OF THE CHURCH

JOSEPH FIELDING SMITH

D1738122

OTHER BOOKS BY TRINA BOICE

Dad's Night: Fantastic Family Nights in 5 Minutes

The Ready Resource for Relief Society
(2012, 2013, 2014)

The Ready Resource for Relief Society, Gospel Principles
(Volumes 1 & 2)

Sabbath Solutions: More Than 350 Ways
You Can Worship on the Lord's Day

Easy Enrichment Ideas: Thinking Outside the Green Gelatin Box

Climbing Family Trees: Whispers in the Leaves

Bright Ideas for Young Women Leaders

Great Ideas for Primary Activity Days

Parties with a Purpose: Exciting Ideas for Ward Activities

Primarily for Cub Scouts

How to Stay UP in a DOWN Economy

"You're What?" 103 Creative Ways to Announce Your Pregnancy

A Gift of Love—A Visual Pun Book of the Heart

The READY RESOURCE

for RELIEF SOCIETY

TEACHINGS OF PRESIDENTS
OF THE CHURCH

JOSEPH FIELDING SMITH

TRINA BOICE

CFI
An Imprint of Cedar Fort, Inc.
Springville, Utah

ISBN 13: 978-1-4621-1353-8

Published by CFI, an imprint of Cedar Fort, Inc., 2373 W. 700 S., Springville, UT, 84663
Distributed by Cedar Fort, Inc., www.cedarfort.com

Cover by Shawnda T. Craig and Rebecca J. Greenwood
Cover design © 2013 Lyle Mortimer
Book design by Rebecca J. Greenwood
Edited and typeset by Emily Chambers and Lindsey Maughan

Printed in the United States of America

10 9 8 7 6 5 4 3 2 1

CONTENTS

CONTENTS

ACKNOWLEDGMENTS

Thank you to Cedar Fort for inviting me to share this book series adventure with them! I want to thank my kind editors, Emily Chambers and Lindsey Maughan, for all of their help with this edition, as well as the wonderful Catherine Christensen for always believing in my book ideas. I'm also grateful to Cedar Fort marketing gurus Kelly Martinez and Rodney Fife for doing such a great job of introducing my words to so many good people.

A big thank you to my wonderfully supportive family for taking care of everything around me while I was busy pounding away at my keyboard! My husband and four sons inspire me to try harder and be better every day. I'm also forever grateful for my extended family's continued enthusiastic support, unconditional love, and kind encouragement.

Thank you to all the faithful members of the Church who valiantly magnify their callings and give of their time and talents to bless those around them. Heavenly Father knows that when we teach others, we learn more deeply ourselves. They say that God loves all people, but especially teachers, because they remind Him of His son!

Not only should we read the scriptures and have a meaningful gospel study plan, but we're commanded to *feast* on the scriptures! It is my hope that this book serves as helpful utensils to enjoy your meal!

INTRODUCTION

The *Ready Resource* for Relief Society and priesthood quorums for 2014 is designed to be a helpful, inspiring resource to make lesson preparation easier and more exciting. You can find the new Church manual for Relief Society and priesthood lessons at:

🙣 http://www.lds.org/manual/teachings-of-the-presidents-of-the-church-joseph-fielding-smith?lang=eng.

The gospel means "good news" and should bring us great joy! Members of the Church of Jesus Christ of Latter-day Saints should be the happiest people around! May you feel the Savior's loving arms enfold you as you teach your dear sisters and feed His sheep.

Each chapter includes hymns appropriate for the lesson, quick summaries of the lesson material, quotes to supplement your class discussions, suggested artwork to display during your presentation, and object lessons to add pizzazz to your student participation. Some new features in this edition of *The Ready Resource for Relief Society* are specific challenges to invite your sisters to apply what they learn to strengthen their spiritual growth, seminary scripture mastery verses, and where to find correlating topics in the Church's *Preach My Gospel* missionary manual. You're not teaching lessons—you're teaching sisters.

Teaching with the Holy Ghost is *the most important* tool in your class. Pray for the Holy Ghost to guide your study preparation before your lesson and for inspiration during your lesson. As you live the commandments and do your utmost to magnify your calling, you will receive personal revelation and direction on how you should share the lessons with your sisters.

The best lessons are not lectures but rather discussions where everyone participates. Try to involve the sisters and encourage them to share their experiences and testimonies of the principles you are teaching. They should leave your class feeling edified, enriched, and excited to live the gospel with joy!

Integrating various learning styles into your lessons improves retention and attention, assists in lesson planning, and inspires participants. Everyone learns differently, so be sure to include variety in your teaching techniques. Try using some of the following ideas during your lessons:

STUDENT CENTERED

Assignments
Brainstorming
Case Study
Crafts
Discussion (general, panel,
    small groups)
Instructional Games

Memorizing
Note Taking
Oral Reading
Role-Playing
Singing
Testimonies
Worksheets

TEACHER CENTERED

Jokes and Puns
Demonstration
Lecture
Surveys
Oral Reading
Catch phrases and Tag Lines
Storytelling

Questions
Summarizing
Personal Emails
Guest Speaker
Dramatization
Personal Photos and Videos
Feedback

MATERIALS CENTERED

Bulletin Board
Chalkboard
Charts and Maps
Social Media
Handouts

Quizzes and Tests
Displays
Flash Cards
Flannel Board
E-books
Mobile Apps

Graphs	Artwork
DVD	Comics
Make Original Films	Pictures and Artwork
Flip Chart	Power Point Presentations
Overhead Transparency	

ARTWORK: Beautiful artwork can teach in a way that words alone cannot, especially for visual learners. Your church building's library may have some larger prints of older pictures, which are numbered. Those numbers will be different than found on pictures in the old Gospel Art Kit (KIT) the Church used to sell in a blue box or in the newer Gospel Art Book (GAB). Picture suggestions in this book will only include references to those two sources: KIT or GAB. However, you can access many pictures on the Church's website at:

ح‍ www.lds.org/media-library/images.

The pictures online are organized into the following categories:

GOSPEL ART
1. Old Testament
2. New Testament
3. Book of Mormon
4. Church History
5. Latter-day Prophets
6. Gospel in Action
JESUS CHRIST
TEMPLES
CHURCH HISTORY
1. Illinois
2. Missouri
3. New York
4. Ohio
5. Pioneer
6. Utah

7. Statues and Plaques
8. Miscellaneous

ILLUSTRATIONS (Perfect for young children)

CHURCH LEADERSHIP (Portraits)

1. First Presidency and Quorum of the Twelve Apostles
2. General Auxiliaries
3. Other General Authorities

BELIEFS AND PRACTICES

SCRIPTURE STUDY

PRIMARY

1. Activity Pages
2. Cutouts
3. Illustrations
4. Line Art

TEACHINGS OF PRESIDENTS OF THE CHURCH

1. George Albert Smith
2. Lorenzo Snow
3. Joseph Field Smith

HISTORICAL

CHILDREN

1. Playing
2. Portraits
3. Miscellaneous

You can purchase a *Gospel Art Book* (GAB) from Church Distribution for only $3.50 at www.ldscatalog.com, which comes as a spiral-bound book containing 137 color pictures. It is also perfect for your own family's Family Home Evening lessons! They are organized into the following categories:

1. Old Testament
2. New Testament
3. Book of Mormon
4. Church History
5. Gospel in Action
6. Latter-day Prophets

Some terrific Church resources that provide excellent artwork on gospel themes can also be found at:

- LDS images: www.images.lds.org
- BYU religious education image archive: http://relarchive.byu .edu/
- Joseph Smith Resource Center (maps, artwork, photos, documents): http://josephsmith.net
- Photographs of scriptural sites: http://scriptures.lds.org /en/bible
- photos/contents
- Photographs of Church History sites: http://scriptures.lds.org /en/chphotos/contents
- Temple photos: http://www.lds.org/temples/home/0,11273 ,1896-1,00.html

Music: Music can effectively teach and invite the Spirit almost better than any other teaching technique. Included with each lesson are suggestions for songs the class can sing or simply learn from by reading the lyrics. Inviting others in your ward to provide special musical numbers during your lessons binds hearts together and uplifts everyone. You can find the LDS hymn book online at:

- http://www.lds.org/churchmusic

You can download songs, listen to them online, and do searches by topics, titles, and even scriptures. You can also use songs from seminary, Young Women's, Primary, and other music that has been published in Church magazines. Also on the Church's website are learning materials, such as how to conduct music, understand symbols and terms, and where to find great ideas to add variety to singing.

Check out these great resources:

- Church Hymns on iTunes: http://itunes.apple.com/us/app/lds -hymns/id332640791?mt=8
- Free LDS musical arrangements: http://freewardchoirmusic .com/
- Free LDS music: http://www.soundsmithmusic.com/

QUOTES: Quotes from Church authorities can be used to inspire the mind and uplift the heart. It's nice to have some quotes written on the board at the front of the room for students to read before class starts to set the tone and to get them thinking about the topic. Some of the suggested handouts in the book use such quotes, but you can also design your own, using your favorite quotes. You can do a search at www.lds .org with a keyword about the topic you're searching for. More can be found online at:

- www.quotegarden.com
- www.thinkexist.com
- www.inspirational-quotes.info
- www.brainyquote.com
- www.quotationspage.com
- www.wisdomquotes.com

ARTICLES: What a blessing it is to read from Church leaders each month in the various Church magazines. Teach your class how to find material they can share with their families during Family Home Evening lessons or to help them prepare sacrament talks in the future. Each lesson in this book includes only a few suggested articles, but there are many more. One of the biggest blessings of preparing your lessons each month will be the focused time you get to spend researching specific gospel topics. You will learn so much more than you'll ever have time to share with your sisters in class on Sunday! Teaching Relief Society is a wonderful excuse to truly immerse yourself in gospel study. Enjoy it!

OBJECT LESSONS: Object lessons capture the students' interest and increase understanding by teaching the concept in a unique way. The Savior often used physical objects that were familiar to His listeners to illustrate simple principles. Each lesson offers ideas for object lessons that could be an effective introduction to the topic or a fun way to keep the class engaged during class time.

VIDEOS: The Church has some excellent videos that can be found and downloaded to your computer. You'll need a projector and either a white wall or screen in order to share them with your class.

An entire new series of Bible videos is currently being filmed in Utah. You can find some beautiful and inspiring videos at:

- www.lds.org/bible-videos

YouTube hosts several "channels" of videos officially released by the Church as well at:

- www.youtube.com/user/MormonMessages
- www.youtube.com/user/LDSPublicAffairs

You'll find a lot of other great LDS videos on YouTube that were uploaded by members of the Church. Many chapels have Internet access, but be sure to do a test run with your equipment before you decide to include videos in your lesson. Your lessons shouldn't be entertainment focused, but spirit focused.

CHALLENGES: Included in this year's edition of *The Ready Resource for Relief Society* is a challenge for the students in each lesson. Perhaps it should be called an "invitation for application." After sharing your lesson material with your class and facilitating inspiring discussions, the sisters then need to *apply* what they've learned after they leave your classroom. If they don't *use* the lesson material to improve their lives and strengthen their testimonies, then they aren't growing spiritually from your efforts. You can offer the suggested challenge, one of your own, or invite the class to choose their own personal goal that will allow them to delve deeper and stretch farther. In the end, we won't be judged by all of the religious trivia we can recite to the Lord at the Judgment Seat, but by the Christlike qualities we have developed. The Lord cares much more about what we are becoming than what we are doing.

SEMINARY SCRIPTURE MASTERY: Parents of seminary students may want to learn some of the same 100 scripture passages that their teens are learning to strengthen their home and family. Teachers can mention which verses correlate with each lesson's topic. What a terrific tool it is to commit scriptures to memory together. You can see all of the seminary manuals and resources at:

ೞ   http://www.lds.org/manual/seminary?lang=eng

PREACH MY GOSPEL: The Church is currently experiencing a wonderful wave of missionaries as the Lord hastens His work. To help the sisters in your ward become more familiar with this missionary service guide, consider including topical passages and talk about how to share your lesson material with non-member friends. You can see a free copy of the manual at:

ೞ   http://www.lds.org/manual/preach-my-gospel-a-guide-to-misisonary-service?lang=eng

RESOURCES: Visit the Church's website section that is dedicated to Relief Society resources at www.lds.org. The section entitled "Sunday Relief Society Meetings" has been created just for you and this sacred calling! The steps suggested for how to prepare a lesson include:

ೞ   Use approved lesson materials.
ೞ   Seek the guidance of the Spirit.
ೞ   Study your lesson in advance.
ೞ   Consider the needs of your sisters.
ೞ   Organize the lesson.
ೞ   Seek the gift of teaching.

Be sure to read about the life of Joseph Fielding Smith in the front of the 2014 Relief Society handbook and share your testimony of this great prophet. The sisters will enjoy seeing pictures of him and getting to know and love him through your lessons this year.

Jesus was the Master Teacher. He still is! He cared deeply about each person He taught. He used variety, honesty, symbolism, storytelling, and challenged His listeners to make specific changes in their lives. The more you study and teach the gospel, the greater your own understanding will be.

Use the scriptures each time you teach and encourage your class to feast from their pages. As you come to love the scriptures, your class will feel that passion and be inspired to feast upon them as well. Your task as a teacher is to invite your sisters to "come unto Christ." In order to do that effectively, you must create an atmosphere where the Holy Ghost will be welcome and able to testify to the hearts of your students. You give voice to the gospel principles taught each week, but it is the testifying power of the Holy Ghost that touches the hearts and transforms lives. May you feel the Spirit guide and direct you as you do your best to magnify this calling.

Articles about teaching with the Spirit:

- Henry B. Eyring, "Rise To Your Call," *Liahona*, Nov. 2002.
- William D. Oswald, "Gospel Teaching—Our Most Important Calling," *Liahona*, Nov. 2008.
- Dallin H. Oaks, "Gospel Teaching," *Ensign*, Nov. 1999.
- Bruce R. McConkie, "The Teacher's Divine Commission," *Ensign*, Apr. 1979.
- David M. McConkie, "Gospel Learning and Teaching," *Liahona*, Nov. 2010.

LESSON ONE
OUR FATHER IN HEAVEN

Music

"Father in Heaven"—*Hymns* #133
"Father in Heaven, We Do Believe"—*Hymns* #180
"God of Our Fathers, We Come Unto Thee"—*Hymns* #76
"I Know My Father Lives"—Children's Songbook #5
"My Heavenly Father Loves Me"—Children's Songbook #228
"O God, The Eternal Father"—*Hymns* #175
"O My Father"—*Hymns* #292

SUMMARY:

There *is* a God! He is a loving Heavenly Father who formed this earth as a school for our learning and progression. He created everything in the universe and knows all things. He has a glorified body of flesh and bones and we are made in His image. We are not only His greatest creation, but we are His sons and daughters. By keeping His commandments we can become like Him.

Because of Joseph Smith's First Vision, the true nature of God has been restored in our day. To exercise real faith in God, we must have a correct understanding of His characteristics. He loves us and has provided the way of redemption so we can return to His presence.

QUOTES

"There is a great difference in believing or knowing that there is a God and in knowing God" (Bernard P. Brockbank, "Knowing God," *Ensign*, July 1972, 121–23).

"We are the children of God. That doctrine is not hidden away in an obscure verse. It is taught over and over again in scripture" (Boyd K. Packer, "The Pattern of Our Parentage," *Ensign,* Nov. 1984, 6).

"Belief in the fact that God exists is of first importance, but it is not all that is necessary in order to exercise an intelligent faith that will lead us back into his presence for eternal life with him" (N. Eldon Tanner, "A Basis for Faith in the Living God," *Ensign,* Nov. 1978, 46–49).

"To follow Christ is to become like Him. It is to learn from His character. As spirit children of our Heavenly Father, we do have the potential to incorporate Christ-like attributes into our life and character" (Dieter F. Uchtdorf, "Developing Christlike Attributes," *Ensign*, Oct. 2008).

GOSPEL ART:

The First Vision—(403 KIT, 90 GAB)
The Brother of Jared Sees the Finger of the Lord—(318 KIT, 85 GAB)

VIDEOS:

- "God is our Father": http://www.lds.org/media-library/video/2011-06-02-god-is-our-father?lang=eng

- "Earthly Father, Heavenly Father": http://www.lds.org/media-library/video/2013-01-002-earthly-father-heavenly-father?lang=eng

- "The Greatest Commandment": http://www.lds.org/media-library/video/2011-10-052-the-greatest-commandment?lang=eng

OBJECT LESSONS:

- Begin by showing a padlock and ask what it can be used for. Ask what good is a lock without a key. Discuss how our lives only find meaning in relationship with our Creator. God has made us and this earth for a purpose. Jesus Christ is the key. Life without God is like a padlock without a key.

- Ask "How many of you would like to see God?" Pass around a mirror and discuss how each one of us is made in His image and how we are truly divine. We can see God's reflection in Jesus; to see God clearly, we need to learn more about the Savior.

- Scramble up the letters to words, using this fun online tool: www.superkids.com/aweb/tools/words/scramble/. Try words like racacrthe (character) or rteytingi (integrity). Have the class try to figure out the words. Later, explain that even if we can disguise our true character from the world, the Lord sees who we really are. Our goal is to become like Him.

CHURCH MAGAZINE ARTICLES:

- Gordon B. Hinckley, "In These Three I Believe," July 2006.
- Bernard P. Brockbank, "Knowing God," July 1972, 121–23.
- Boyd K. Packer, "The Pattern of Our Parentage," November 1984, 66–69.
- N. Eldon Tanner, "A Basis for Faith in the Living God," November
- 1978, 46–49.

CHALLENGE:

Memorize all of the verses of "I Am A Child of God."
Spend fifteen minutes in prayer with Heavenly Father. Talk less and listen more.

SEMINARY SCRIPTURE MASTERY:

3 Nephi 27:27

Moses 1:39

Genesis 1:26–27

Exodus 20:3–17

Exodus 33:11

Deuteronomy 7:3–4

Joshua 24:15

1 Samuel 16:7

Acts 7:55–56

D&C 130:22–23

PREACH MY GOSPEL:

Pages 31–32, 37, 48

"We are the children of God.
That doctrine is not hidden away in
an obscure verse. It is taught over
and over again in scripture."
—Boyd K. Packer, "The Pattern of Our Parentage," *Ensign,* Nov. 1984

"We are the children of God.
That doctrine is not hidden away in
an obscure verse. It is taught over
and over again in scripture."
—Boyd K. Packer, "The Pattern of Our Parentage," *Ensign,* Nov. 1984

OUR SAVIOR, JESUS CHRIST

Music

"Christ The Lord Is Risen Today"—*Hymns* #200
"God Loved Us, So He Sent His Son"—*Hymns* #187
"I Believe In Christ"—*Hymns* #134
"In Humility, Our Savior"—*Hymns* #172
"Our Savior's Love"—*Hymns* #113

SUMMARY:

Jesus Christ is the Only Begotten Son of God and the Savior of the world. He was chosen and foreordained to come to earth to atone for our sins and teach us how to return to our Heavenly Father. Our faith is built upon the Savior's atoning sacrifice.

The most important event in the history of mankind was when the Savior was crucified for the world. Jesus Christ's Atonement took place in the Garden of Gethsemane and on the cross at Calvary. His redeeming sacrifice was necessary to ransom all people from the physical and spiritual effects of the Fall. Because of His merciful gift, everyone has the opportunity to repent, be forgiven of their sins, and be resurrected.

The Savior was the only one capable of making a perfect atonement for all humankind, because He is the only Son of God in the flesh and He was completely obedient and without sin. To thank Him for paying our spiritual and physical debts, we must show faith in Him, repent, be baptized, and follow Him. By following Jesus Christ, we can return to live with our eternal Father. He has revealed Himself in our dispensation, and we can build a testimony of Him through scripture study, prayer, and following His example.

QUOTES:

"The stories of Jesus can be like a rushing wind across the embers of faith in the hearts of our children. Jesus said 'I am the way, the truth, and the life.' The stories of Jesus shared over and over bring faith in the Lord Jesus Christ and strength to the foundation of testimony. Can you think of a more valuable gift for our children?" (Neil L. Andersen, "Tell Me the Stories of Jesus," *Ensign*, May 2010).

"Each of us has the responsibility to know the Lord, love Him, follow Him, serve Him, teach and testify of Him" (Russell M. Nelson, "Jesus the Christ: Our Master and More," *Ensign*, Apr. 2000, 4–17).

"The soul that comes unto Christ dwells within a personal fortress, a veritable palace of perfect peace" (Jeffrey R. Holland, "Come unto Me," *Ensign*, Apr. 1998, 16–23).

"The Redeemer loves you and will help you do the essential things that bring happiness now and forever" (Richard G. Scott, "Jesus Christ, Our Redeemer," *Ensign*, May 1997, 53–54, 59).

"Ever and always [the Atonement] offers amnesty from transgression and from death if we will but repent. . . . Repentance is the key with which we can unlock the prison from inside . . . , and agency is ours to use it" (Boyd K. Packer, "Atonement, Agency, Accountability," *Ensign*, May 1988, 69–72).

"The Lord's Atonement is the most transcendent event that ever has or ever will occur, from Creation's dawn through all the ages of a never-ending eternity" (Bruce R. McConkie, "The Purifying Power of Gethsemane," *Ensign*, May 1985, 9–11).

"To follow Christ is to become like Him. It is to learn from His character. As spirit children of our Heavenly Father, we do have the potential to incorporate Christlike attributes into our life and character" (Dieter F. Uchtdorf, "Developing Christlike Attributes," *Ensign*, Oct. 2008).

GOSPEL ART:

Isaiah Writes of Christ's Birth—(113 KIT, 22 GAB)
The Nativity—(201 KIT, 30 GAB)
Boy Jesus in the Temple—(205 KIT, 34 GAB)
Childhood of Jesus Christ—(206 KIT)
John the Baptist Baptizing Jesus—(208 KIT, 35 GAB)
Calling of the Fishermen—(209 KIT, 37 GAB)
Christ Ordaining the Apostles—(211 KIT, 38 GAB)
Sermon on the Mount—(212 KIT, 39 GAB)
Christ Healing a Blind Man—(213 KIT)
Stilling the Storm—(214 KIT)
Jesus Blessing Jairus's Daughter—(215 KIT, 41 GAB)
Christ and the Children—(216 KIT)
Triumphal Entry—(223 KIT, 50 GAB)
Jesus Washing the Apostles' Feet—(226 KIT, 55 GAB)
Jesus Praying in Gethsemane—(227 KIT, 56 GAB)
The Betrayal of Jesus—(228 KIT)
The Crucifixion—(230 KIT, 57 GAB)
Jesus' Tomb—(232 KIT, 58 GAB)
Mary and the Resurrected Lord—(233 KIT, 59 GAB)
Jesus Shows His Wounds—(234 KIT, 60 GAB)
Go Ye Therefore—(235 KIT, 61 GAB)
The Ascension of Jesus—(236 KIT, 62 GAB)
Jesus at the Door—(237 KIT, 65 GAB)
The Second Coming—(238 KIT, 66 GAB)
The Resurrected Jesus Christ—(239 KIT, 66 GAB)
Christ Walking on the Water—(243 KIT, 43 GAB)
Christ and the Rich Young Ruler—(244 KIT, 48 GAB)

The Empty Tomb—(245 KIT)
Jesus Christ Appears to the Nephites—(315 KIT, 82 GAB)
Christ and Children from Around the World—(608 KIT)
Jesus Blesses the Nephite Children—(84 GAB)

VIDEOS:

There are *many* videos to choose from in the Church's new Bible Videos about the Life of Jesus Christ found at:

- http://www.lds.org/media-library/video/bible-videos-the-life-of-jesus-christ?lang-eng

- "Are we Christians?": http://www.lds.org/media-library/video/2009-02-07-are-we-christians?lang=eng

- "Jesus Christ Suffered for us": http://www.lds.org/media-library/video/2010-05-1150-jesus-christ-suffered-for-is?lang=eng

- "He is Risen": http://www.lds.org/media-library/video/2011-10-025-he-is-risen?lang=eng

OBJECT LESSONS:

- Pass out pictures of Jesus Christ and ask class members to share what they know about the picture they're holding. This simple exercise becomes an instant testimony meeting as the sisters share how they feel about the Savior and the events of His life.

- Show the class some different kinds of keys: old-fashioned ones, key rings, hotel card keys, etc. Explain how the keys let you into appealing locations: fancy hotel rooms, luxury vehicles, bank safes and so on. Some people judge their lives by the keys they possess: an education is the key to a good career. A car is a key to freedom. A good job is the key to power and wealth. A key to a large home represents success and security. There is only one key that opens the most important destination of all: Jesus Christ is the key to eternal life with Father in Heaven!

- Show objects that the class has to relate to Jesus Christ
  - Porch light: serves as a beacon to help us find our way home
  - Campfire: provides warmth and comfort
  - Lighthouse: Offers light in the darkness, offers perspective in the storm
  - Night light: banishes darkness and eliminates fear
  - Car headlights: lets us know where we are heading
  - Lights in a movie theater: a guide that can be followed
  - Light bulb: inspires us and brings us new light and understanding

- Ask someone in the class to put on a sock. Hand the volunteer a muddy sock. The volunteer will probably not want to touch the dirty sock, so ask her what could be done to make her willing. Tell her you'll take the muddy sock and give her a clean, new one. The Savior took upon Himself all of our dirty sins and gave us each a clean sock to wear when we return to our Father in Heaven so that we will be clean from the sins of the world.

- Pass around a beautiful rose, but with the thorns still intact. Talk about how fragrant and pleasing it is. Next, bruise some of the rose petals and point out the thorns. Jesus' body was bruised for our iniquities and a crown of thorns was placed on his head. Now ask someone to be a timekeeper and someone else to take the rose petals off the stem as fast as possible. Ask for another volunteer and timekeeper. Say "Okay, let's see if you can beat that time. Ready? Let's see you put it back together!" No matter how hard we try, we can't rebuild a rose, but God can not only do that, but he can also restore life through Jesus Christ. We are even more beautiful than a rose and will all be resurrected because with God, all things are possible!

❧ Ask for a volunteer to stand in a square that is marked on the floor with masking tape. Show her a candy bar on the table and tell her she can have it only if she can reach it without leaving the square. Ask for another volunteer to help her. That's what the Savior did for us . . . He gave us the sweet gift of eternal life.

ARTICLES:

❧ Ezra Taft Benson, "Five Marks of the Divinity of Jesus Christ," *Ensign*, December 2001.

❧ Ezra Taft Benson, "Jesus Christ: Our Savior and Redeemer," *Ensign*, June 1990.

❧ Russell M. Nelson, "Jesus the Christ: Our Master and More," *Ensign*, April 2000.

❧ Orson F. Whitney, "The Divinity of Jesus Christ," *Ensign*, December 2003.

❧ M. Russell Ballard, "The Atonement and the Value of One Soul," *Ensign*, May 2004.

❧ Cecil O. Samuelson Jr., "What Does the Atonement Mean to You?" *Ensign*, Apr. 2009.

❧ Marion G. Romney, "Christ's Atonement: The Gift Supreme," *Ensign*, Dec. 1973.

❧ James E. Faust, "The Atonement: Our Greatest Hope," *Ensign*, Nov. 2001.

CHALLENGE:

Write your testimony of Jesus Christ in your journal and share it with your family. Write it in a Book of Mormon and share it with a non-member.

SEMINARY SCRIPTURE MASTERY:

Helaman 5:12
3 Nephi 27:27
Genesis 1:26–27
Job 19:25–26
Isaiah 53:3–5
Matthew 16:15–19
Luke 24:36–39

John 3:5
John 17:3
Acts 7:55–56
1 Corinthians 15:20–22
D&C 19:16–19
D&C 76:22–24
D&C 130:22–23

PREACH MY GOSPEL:

Pages 34, 37, 47–48, 51–52, 60–61

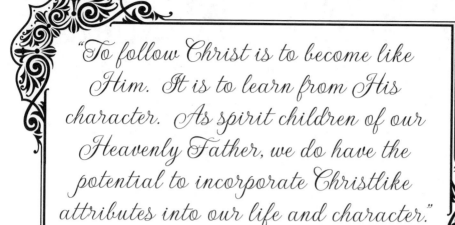

"To follow Christ is to become like Him. It is to learn from His character. As spirit children of our Heavenly Father, we do have the potential to incorporate Christlike attributes into our life and character."

—Dieter F. Uchtdorf, "Developing Christlike Attributes,"
Ensign, Oct. 2008

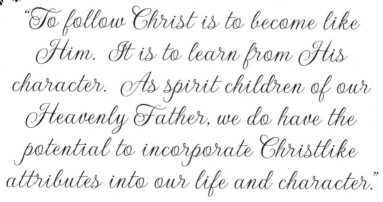

"To follow Christ is to become like Him. It is to learn from His character. As spirit children of our Heavenly Father, we do have the potential to incorporate Christlike attributes into our life and character."

—Dieter F. Uchtdorf, "Developing Christlike Attributes,"
Ensign, Oct. 2008

THE PLAN OF SALVATION

Music

"Know This, That Every Soul Is Free"—*Hymns #240*
"Lord, Accept into They Kingdom"—*Hymns #236*
"Testimony"—*Hymns #236*
"We Are Marching On to Glory"—*Hymns #225*
"We are Sowing"—*Hymns #216*

SUMMARY:

This earth life is a part of eternity. We lived before we arrived here, and we have somewhere wonderful to go after this mortal experience. What a comfort it is to know that death is only an end of this part of our immortal journey. Our earth life is to prepare us not to die, but to live with our Heavenly Father for eternity. When we first heard this plan in our premortal existence, we shouted for joy! Knowing that everything we do and learn in life will enhance our experience after we leave this earth should inspire us to do our best while we are here.

Also called *the plan of happiness*, the plan of salvation has been designed to make us happy! Thanks to the resurrection of Jesus Christ, everyone will have an opportunity to step beyond death and continue living. The Fall of Adam and Eve was part of this plan and began our journey into mortality where we work toward eternal salvation. After our mortal bodies have been purified, everyone will be resurrected and our immortal spirits will be housed in them again to live forever. This mortal life is only a temporary home. The faithful will return home to live in the presence of our loving Heavenly Father.

QUOTES:

"Thus we see in the eternal plan of our Father that His love has no bounds. Every one of His children is included. All men have the same origin and equal possibility to fulfill their eternal destiny" (L. Tom Perry, "The Plan of Salvation," *Ensign*, Nov. 2006).

"Life never was intended to be easy. Rather, it is a period of proving and growth. It is interwoven with difficulties, challenges, and burdens. We are immersed in a sea of persistent, worldly pressures that could destroy our happiness. Yet these very forces, if squarely faced, provide opportunity for tremendous personal growth and development. The conquering of adversity produces strength of character, forges self-confidence, engenders self-respect, and assures success in righteous endeavor" (Richard G. Scott, "The Plan of Happiness and Exaltation," *Ensign*, Nov. 1981).

"Eternal life is to live with our Father and with our families forevermore. Should not this promise be the greatest incentive to do the best within our reach and give the best of ourselves in pursuit of what has been promised to us?" (Jorge F. Zeballos, "Attempting the Impossible," *Ensign*, Nov. 2009, 33).

"When we understand the plan of salvation, we also understand the purpose and effect of the commandments God has given His children" (Dallin H. Oaks, "The Great Plan of Happiness," *Ensign*, Nov. 1993, 72–75).

"The plan of salvation . . . comprises all of the laws, ordinances, principles, and doctrines required to complete our mortal journey and progress to a state of exaltation enjoyed by our Father in Heaven" (Duane B. Gerrard, "The Plan of Salvation: A Flight Plan for Life," *Ensign*, Nov. 1997, 77–78).

GOSPEL ART:

Isaiah Writes of Christ's Birth—(113 KIT, 22 GAB)

Jesus Blessing Jairus's Daughter—(215 KIT, 41 GAB)

The Crucifixion—(230 KIT, 57 GAB)

The Ascension of Jesus—(236 KIT, 62 GAB)

The Second Coming—(238 KIT, 66 GAB)

The Resurrected Jesus Christ—(239 KIT)

The Empty Tomb—(245 KIT)

Jesus Christ Appears to the Nephites—(315 KIT, 82 GAB)

The Brother of Jared Sees the Finger of the Lord—(318 KIT, 85 GAB)

The First Vision—(403 KIT, 90 GAB)

Moroni Appears to Joseph Smith in His Room—(404 KIT, 91 GAB)

John the Baptist Conferring the Aaronic Priesthood—(407 KIT, 93 GAB)

Melchizedek Priesthood Restoration—(408 KIT, 94 GAB)

Elijah Restores the Power to Seal Families for Eternity—(417 KIT, 95 GAB)

Kirtland Temple—(500 KIT, 117 GAB)

Nauvoo Illinois Temple—(510 KIT, 118 GAB)

Salt Lake Temple—(502 KIT, 119 GAB)

Temple Baptismal Font—(504 KIT, 121 GAB)

The World—(600 KIT)

Young Couple Going to the Temple—(609 KIT, 120 GAB)

VIDEOS:

- "The Plan of Salvation": http://lds.org/library/display/0,4945,6635-1-4786-3,00.html

- "Preparation for the Afterlife": http://lds.org/media-library/video/our-values?lang=eng

- "What Happens When I Die?": http://lds.org/media-library/video/our-faith?lang=eng

- "Chapter 1: Before the Old Testament": http://lds.org/media-library/video/old-testament-stories?lang=eng

- "Man's Search for Happiness": http://www.youtube.com/watch?v=ojX172jFp-l

- "Film of Man's Search for Happiness": http://www.youtube.com/watch?v=cNm1enzlwvo

OBJECT LESSONS:

- Show a picture of a human body and talk about all of the things we need to do to take care of its physical nature. Then, talk about the spiritual body and what is required to keep it healthy and functioning correctly. For example:
  - Heart: Eat healthy and exercise (physical)—Serve and love (spiritual)
  - Eyes: Food, exercise, sleep (physical)—Read the scriptures and pray (spiritual)
  - Ears: Clean them, be careful of loud sounds (physical)—Listen to the Lord and His servants

- Hang a clothes line across the front of the classroom, placing signs that identify the Pre-mortal World, Mortality, Death, Spirit Prison, Paradise, the Final Judgment, and the three degrees of glory. Create paper dolls that could be hung along the eternal continuum, explaining different kinds of scenarios for each "doll's" life, such as when they lived and died, and what kind of life they lived. Have the class decide where to hang the paper dolls.

- Ask the class if they would like to eat a cookie now or have 5 cookies in half an hour. Explain that heaven is like that. Although the things of this world seem very appealing, our heavenly reward is much better. We need to be patient and wait because there is a delicious banquet in store for us after this earth life. Serve cookies during the class.

ARTICLES:

- John M. Madsen, "Eternal Life through Jesus Christ," *Ensign*, July 2002.
- Delbert L. Stapley, "The Path to Eternal Life," *Ensign*, Jan. 1974.
- Russell M. Nelson, "Life After Life," *Ensign*, May 1987.
- Joseph B. Wirthlin, "What Is the Difference Between Immortality and Eternal Life?" *New Era*, Nov. 2006.
- Richard G. Scott, "The Joy of Living the Great Plan of Happiness," *Ensign*, Nov. 1996, 73–75.
- Duane B. Gerrard, "The Plan of Salvation: A Flight Plan for Life," *Ensign*, Nov. 1997, 77–78.
- Neal A. Maxwell, "The Great Plan of the Eternal God," *Ensign*, May 1984, 21–23.
- Dallin H. Oaks, "The Great Plan of Happiness," *Ensign*, Nov. 1993, 72–75.

CHALLENGE:

Begin a Gratitude Journal where you write down all of the things and experiences you're grateful for in this mortal life. This record can be a great reminder to you that, even with trials and hardships, mortal life can be a wonderful experience. We are spiritual beings having a mortal experience, not mortal beings having spiritual experiences.

SEMINARY SCRIPTURE MASTERY:

2 Nephi 2:25	Moses 1:39
2 Nephi 2:27	Abraham 3:22–23
Alma 41:10	Genesis 1:26–27
Helaman 5:12	Isaiah 53:3–5
3 Nephi 27:27	Acts 7:55–56

1 Corinthians 15:20–22   D&C 130:18–19
1 Corinthians 15:40–42   D&C 131:1–4
Revelation 20:12–13   D&C 137:7–10

PREACH MY GOSPEL:

Pages 47–54

"THE CONQUERING OF ADVERSITY PRODUCES STRENGTH OF CHARACTER, FORGES SELF-CONFIDENCE, ENGENDERS SELF-RESPECT, AND ASSURES SUCCESS IN RIGHTEOUS ENDEAVOR."
—Richard G. Scott, "The Plan of Happiness and Exaltation," *Ensign*, Nov. 1981

"THE CONQUERING OF ADVERSITY PRODUCES STRENGTH OF CHARACTER, FORGES SELF-CONFIDENCE, ENGENDERS SELF-RESPECT, AND ASSURES SUCCESS IN RIGHTEOUS ENDEAVOR."
—Richard G. Scott, "The Plan of Happiness and Exaltation," *Ensign*, Nov. 1981

STRENGTHENING AND PRESERVING THE FAMILY

Music

"Families Can Be Together Forever"—*Hymns #300*
"Home Can Be a Heaven on Earth"—*Hymns #298*
"O My Father"—*Hymns #292*
"Teach Me to Walk in the Light"—*Hymns #304*

SUMMARY:

Life is eternal. We come from heavenly parents who are waiting for us to return to them, having learned the lessons of life and gained the characteristics they possess. To remind us of our heavenly home, we are given the opportunity to be parents here on earth and raise a family of our own. Salvation is a family affair. The family is the most important unit in time and eternity. We are placed here as families to learn how to care for one another, so that we may all safely return home together. Temple marriage is a covenant partnership with the Lord that allows us to seal souls together as eternal families.

Each member of the family plays an important role in returning to live with our heavenly parents. Fathers are to provide, protect and preside over families. Mothers are divinely designed to bear and nurture children. Children are commanded to honor and obey their parents. If everyone takes responsibility for a happy family, they can all experience a little bit of heaven on earth.

Be sensitive to the sisters in the class who may have never married, lost a spouse, or divorced. Remind them the Lord has promised a fulness of blessings to all those who are faithful.

QUOTES:

"Without proper and successful marriage, one will never be exalted" (Spencer W. Kimball, "Marriage and Divorce," Salt Lake City: Deseret Book, 1976, 24).

"In light of the ultimate purpose of the great plan of happiness, I believe that the ultimate treasures on earth and in heaven are our children and our posterity" (Dallin H. Oaks, "The Great Plan of Happiness," *Ensign*, Oct. 1993).

"Under the plan of heaven, the husband and the wife walk side by side as companions, neither one ahead of the other, but a daughter of God and a son of God walking side by side. Let your families be families of love and peace and happiness. Gather your children around you and have your family home evenings, teach your children the ways of the Lord, read to them from the scriptures, and let them come to know the great truths of the eternal gospel as set forth in these words of the Almighty" ("Selections from Addresses of President Gordon B. Hinckley," *Ensign*, Mar. 2001, 64).

"Our family is the focus of our greatest work and joy in this life; so will it be throughout all eternity" (Russell M. Nelson, "Set in Order Thy House," *Liahona*, Jan. 2002, 80–83).

"The key to strengthening our families is having the Spirit of the Lord come into our homes. The goal of our families is to be on the strait and narrow path" (Robert D. Hales, "Strengthening Families: Our Sacred Duty," *Liahona*, July 1999, 37–40).

"The family unit is fundamental not only to society and to the Church but [also] to our hope for eternal life" (Henry B. Eyring, "The Family," *Liahona*, Oct. 1998, 12–23).

GOSPEL ART:

Jesus Christ—(240 KIT, 1 GAB)
Adam and Eve Kneeling at an Altar—(4 KIT, 4 GAB)
Adam and Eve Teaching Their Children—(5 KIT, 5 GAB)
Jacob Blessing His Sons—(12 GAB)
Lehi's Dream—(69 GAB)
Elijah Appearing in the Kirtland Temple—(95 GAB)
Young Couple Going to the Temple—(120 GAB)

VIDEOS:

- "Until We Meet Again": www.lds.org/ldsorg/v/index.jsp?vgnextoid=bd163ca6e9aa3210VgnVCM1000003a94610aRCRD&locale=0

- "The Blessings of the Temple": www.lds.org/ldsorg/v/index.jsp?vgnextoid=bd163ca6e9aa3210VgnVCM1000003a94610aRCRD&locale=0

- "Faith and Families": www.lds.org/ldsorg/v/index.jsp?locale=0&vgnextoid=22dfd7256ec8b010VgnVCM1000004d82620aRCRD&year=2005

- "Marriage and Divorce": www.lds.org/ldsorg/v/index.jsp?vgnextoid=bd163ca6e9aa3210VgnVCM1000003a94610aRCRD&locale=0

OBJECT LESSONS:

- Get two large envelopes, one with a picture of a temple on the outside. Ask a volunteer to place paper dolls inside the two envelopes, creating families out of the pictures. Lick the envelope that has the picture of a temple on the outside. Talk about life's challenges that can tear us apart and then put the two envelopes upside down, shaking the contents around. The family that has been sealed together will stay together, but the pictures of the other family will all fall out of the envelope.

❧ Pass out copies of the "Proclamation on the Family" to everyone in the class and have them color and decorate them during your lesson.

❧ Place a candy bar on each side of the room. Invite two sisters to come up and link arms, back to back. Tell them they have 10 seconds to get their respective candy bar. When you say, "Go!" they will each begin pulling the other one in the opposite direction; one will either get their candy bar or neither will. Our goal as a family is to return to our heavenly home in tact and it will take all of us working together to accomplish.

❧ Place a stalk of celery in a glass of colored water a few days prior to your lesson. The food coloring in the water will actually draw up into the celery. Show the class your visual aid and ask them to draw analogies between the celery, food coloring and our parenting skills. Children literally soak up what is around them in the home: anger, love, gospel study, apathy, etc. We need to constantly expose our children to positive behaviors in order for them to absorb the gospel.

ARTICLES:

❧ Robert D. Hales, "The Eternal Family," *Ensign*, Nov. 1996, 64–67.
❧ Henry B. Eyring, "The Family," *Ensign*, Feb. 1998, 10–18.
❧ L. Tom Perry, "The Importance of the Family," *Ensign*, May 2003, 40–43.

- Spencer W. Kimball, "Living the Gospel in the Home," *Ensign*, May 1978.
- Spencer W. Kimball, "The Importance of Celestial Marriage," *Ensign*, Oct. 1979, 2–6.
- Bruce C. Hafen, "Covenant Marriage," *Ensign*, Nov. 1996, 26–28.
- F. Burton Howard, "Eternal Marriage," *Ensign*, May 2003, 92–94.

CHALLENGE:

Write down the names of everyone in your family and a list of things you can do to serve them and help them reach their personal goals.

SEMINARY SCRIPTURE MASTERY:

Ether 12:27

Moroni 7:45

2 Timothy 3:1–5

D&C 14:7

D&C 58:26–27

D&C 88:123–24

D&C 131:1–4

PREACH MY GOSPEL:

Pages 3, 32, 85, 159–164

"OUR FAMILY IS THE FOCUS OF OUR GREATEST WORK AND JOY IN THIS LIFE; SO WILL IT BE THROUGHOUT ALL ETERNITY."

—Russell M. Nelson, "Set in Order Thy House," *Liahona,* Jan. 2002

"OUR FAMILY IS THE FOCUS OF OUR GREATEST WORK AND JOY IN THIS LIFE; SO WILL IT BE THROUGHOUT ALL ETERNITY."

—Russell M. Nelson, "Set in Order Thy House," *Liahona,* Jan. 2002

"OUR FAMILY IS THE FOCUS OF OUR GREATEST WORK AND JOY IN THIS LIFE; SO WILL IT BE THROUGHOUT ALL ETERNITY."

—Russell M. Nelson, "Set in Order Thy House," *Liahona,* Jan. 2002

LESSON FIVE
FAITH AND REPENTANCE

Music

"Go Forth With Faith"—*Hymns* #263
"Faith of Our Fathers"—*Hymns* #84
"When Faith Endures"—*Hymns* #128
"True to the Faith"—*Hymns* #254
"With Humble Heart"—*Hymns* #171
"Savior, Redeemer of My Soul"—*Hymns* #112
"Come Unto Jesus"—*Hymns* #117

SUMMARY:

The first principle of the gospel is faith in the Lord Jesus Christ. Faith is believing in Him with our spiritual eyes when we haven't seen Him with our physical eyes. It is a principle of action that compels us to pray, repent, be obedient, and trust in His promises. We increase our faith by testing and studying His words. Faith has power to move mountains, perform miracles, and prove us worthy to see God.

Repentance is the second principle of the gospel and is essential to our salvation and exaltation. We all sin when we are less than perfect in our obedience to God's laws. Only Jesus Christ was without sin. A merciful Father in Heaven sent His son to atone for our sins in order that we may return to His presence. Repentance is the process that allows us to receive forgiveness and grow spiritually. The steps of repentance include recognizing our error, feeling sorrow for our sin, forsaking our bad behavior, confessing our sins to the Lord's servant, and making restitution to right the wrong. We are also commanded to forgive others, to not procrastinate our repentance, and to raise a voice of warning to the world.

QUOTES:

"No part of walking by faith is more difficult than walking the road of repentance. However, with 'faith unto repentance,' we can push roadblocks out of the way, moving forward to beg God for mercy" (Neal A. Maxwell, "Repentance," *Ensign*, Nov. 1991).

"This is my prayer for all of us—'Lord, increase our faith.' Increase our faith to bridge the chasms of uncertainty and doubt. . . . Grant us faith to look beyond the problems of the moment to the miracles of the future. . . . Give us faith to do what is right and let the consequence follow" (Gordon B. Hinckley, "Lord, Increase Our Faith," *Ensign*, Nov. 1987, 52–53).

"Only faith in the Lord Jesus Christ and His Atonement can bring us peace, hope, and understanding" (Robert D. Hales, "Finding Faith in the Lord Jesus Christ," *Ensign*, Nov. 2004, 70–73).

"We promote the process of strengthening our faith when we do what is right—increased faith always follows" (L. Whitney Clayton, "Help Thou Mine Unbelief," *Ensign*, Nov. 2001, 28–29).

"Faith in Jesus Christ takes us beyond mere acceptance of the Savior's identity and existence. It includes having complete confidence in His infinite and eternal redemptive power" (James O. Mason, "Faith in Jesus Christ," *Ensign*, Apr. 2001, 22–27).

"The promise of the Lord is that He will cleanse our garments with His blood. . . . He can redeem us from our personal fall" (Lynn A. Mickelsen, "The Atonement, Repentance, and Dirty Linen," *Ensign*, Nov. 2003, 10–13).

"The steps of repentance . . . produce purity, peace of mind, self-respect, hope, and finally, a new person with a renewed life and abundance of opportunity" (Richard G. Scott, "Finding Forgiveness," *Ensign*, May 1995, 75–77).

"Repentance is timeless. The evidence of repentance is transformation" (Spencer W. Kimball, "What Is True Repentance?" *New Era*, May 1974, 4–7).

"What a wonderful gift the Savior offers—to feel the joy of being free from sin" (Neil L. Andersen, "Clean Again!" *New Era*, Apr. 1997, 4–7).

GOSPEL ART:

The Prodigal Son—(220 KIT)
Jesus Praying in Gethsemane—(227 KIT, 56 GAB)
The Crucifixion—(230 KIT, 57 GAB)
Jesus at the Door—(237 KIT, 65 GAB)
The Resurrected Jesus Christ—(239 KIT)
Jesus the Christ—(240 KIT, 1 GAB)
Enos Praying—(305 KIT, 72 GAB)
The Anti-Nephi-Lehies Burying Their Swords—(311 KIT)
Conversion of Alma the Younger—(321 KIT, 77 GAB)
The Ten Commandments—(14 GAB)
Abraham Taking Isaac to Be Sacrificed—(105 KIT, 9 GAB)
Three Men in the Fiery Furnace—(116 KIT, 25 GAB)
Daniel in the Lions' Den—(117 KIT, 26 GAB)
Moses and the Brass Serpent—(123 KIT, 16 GAB)
Christ Healing a Blind Man—(213 KIT, 42 GAB)
Jesus Blessing Jairus's Daughter –(215 KIT, 41 GAB)
Two Thousand Young Warriors—(313 KIT, 80 GAB)
The Brother of Jared Sees the Finger of the Lord—(318 KIT, 85 GAB)
The Articles of Faith—(618 KIT)

VIDEOS:

- "The Transforming Power of Faith and Character," Richard G. Scott: http://www.lds.org/media-library/video/general-conference -october-2010?lang=eng&query=character#2010-10-2080-elder -richard-g-scott

- "We Believe: Theme Song": http://lds.org/media-library/video /strength-of-youth-media?lang=eng

- "Finding Faith in Christ": http://lds.org/media-library/video /feature-films?lang=eng

- "Waiting on Our Road to Damascus": http://mormonchannel .org/video?v=1452683656001

OBJECT LESSONS:

- Pass out some baby food jars filled with whipping cream. Ask the class if they have faith that the cream can turn into butter. Explain that faith isn't just believing in something, but that it leads to action. Have the class shake the jars during the lesson until the cream turns into sweet butter. Talk about how faith requires patience and waiting, because we often don't see the reward until much later. Before the lesson ends, pass out blueberry muffins that the butter can be served on for all to enjoy.

- Hand each person in class a clear marble and ask them to look through it. The image of whatever they're looking at will be upside down. Share Romans 12:2 (And be not conformed to this world: but be ye transformed by the renewing of your mind, that ye may prove what is that good, and acceptable, and perfect, will of God.) In today's world where society calls good evil and evil good, we can have faith that when Christ comes again, all will be transformed to that which is right. Having faith in Jesus Christ helps us see correctly with our spiritual eyes.

❧ Show the class a checkerboard with 1 grain of wheat on the first square, 2 on the second, 4 on the third, and 8, 16, 32, 64, 128, etc. Ask the class "At this rate of doubling every square, how much grain would you have on the checkerboard by the time you reach the 64th square?" Let the class guess and tell them the correct answer is enough grain to cover the entire subcontinent of India 50 feet deep! Each square represents some area of their life where they need to trust God. Talk about how our faith may start out small, but as God uses it, the end result can be miraculous and quite powerful.

❧ Hand out various objects to class members and have them explain how those items are like repentance. Easy objects to use include:
  ✦ soap
  ✦ pencil eraser
  ✦ knotted rope
  ✦ calculator
  ✦ sponge

❧ Start with a jar filled with clear water and label it "us." Next, take food coloring, labeled "sin" and add a drop each time you discuss various sins. Talk about the Atonement as you pour some bleach, labeled "ATONEMENT" into the jar. Stir the water, which represents REPENTANCE and the class should see that the water clears up and is "clean" like before.

❧ Wear a long-sleeved, white, buttoned-up shirt that has holes in it, dirt marks, food smears and words that say things like: drugs, profanity, gossip, anger, stealing, lying, disobedience, etc. When you talk about repentance, take that shirt off, revealing a clean, white shirt underneath.

❧ Invite several sisters to bring items to display that represent things they're currently studying about and ask them to share with the class a few things they've learned. Have them share how their learning has increased their faith.

❧ Ask someone to lift various sizes of weights. Some objects should be light and easy, and others should be quite difficult to lift. Ask the sisters what they could do to help her without touching her weights. Ask how building faith is like building muscle. Talk about what kind of learning could be done to strengthen faith. Ask how our faith can help us lift our heavy burdens in life. Compare the light weights with leisure learning; contrast that with the heavier weights which represent true study of topics.

ARTICLES:

❧ Gordon B. Hinckley, "Faith: The Essence of True Religion," *Ensign*, Oct. 1995.

❧ Russell M. Nelson, "Faith in Jesus Christ," *Ensign*, Mar. 2008.

❧ Robert D. Hales, "Finding Faith in the Lord Jesus Christ," *Ensign*, Nov. 2004.

❧ Spencer W. Kimball, "The Gospel of Repentance," *Ensign*, Oct. 1982.

❧ Ezra Taft Benson, "Cleansing the Inner Vessel." *Ensign*, May 1986.

❧ Boyd K. Packer, "I Will Remember Your Sins No More," *Ensign*, May 2006.

❧ Russell M. Nelson, "Jesus Christ—the Master Healer," *Ensign*, Nov. 2005.

❧ David A. Bednar, "Clean Hands and a Pure Heart," *Ensign*, Nov. 2007.

CHALLENGE:

Write a list of all the things that build your faith. Begin doing one of the things on your list that you haven't included in your daily life. Repent from something today that you're currently struggling with.

SEMINARY SCRIPTURE MASTERY:

2 Nephi 2:27	Proverbs 3:5–6
2 Nephi 28:7–9	Isaiah 1:18
Mosiah 4:30	Isaiah 55:8–9
Alma 32:21	John 14:15
Alma 34:32–34	James 1:5–6
Alma 41:10	James 2:17–18
Ether 12:6	D&C 19:16–19
Genesis 39:9	D&C 58:42–43
Exodus 20:3–17	D&C 59:9–10
Psalm 24:3–4	D&C 82:3

PREACH MY GOSPEL:

Pages 49–50, 62–63, 93–95, 155, 187–190, 195

"*Faith in Jesus Christ takes us beyond mere acceptance of the Savior's identity and existence. It includes having complete confidence in His infinite and eternal redemptive power.*"

—James O. Mason, "Faith in Jesus Christ," *Ensign*, Apr. 2001, 22–27

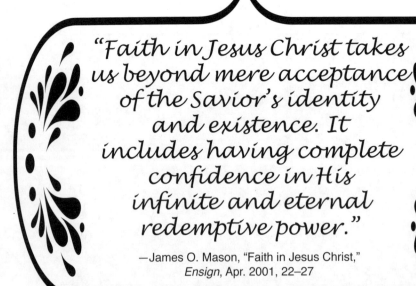

"*Faith in Jesus Christ takes us beyond mere acceptance of the Savior's identity and existence. It includes having complete confidence in His infinite and eternal redemptive power.*"

—James O. Mason, "Faith in Jesus Christ," *Ensign*, Apr. 2001, 22–27

THE SIGNIFICANCE OF THE SACRAMENT

Music

"As Now We Take the Sacrament"—*Hymns* #169

"Before I Take the Sacrament"—Children's Songbook #73

"Father in Heaven, We Do Believe"—*Hymns* #180

"Gently Raise the Sacred Strain"—*Hymns* #146

"In Memory of the Crucified"—*Hymns* #190

"The Sacrament"—Children's Songbook #72

SUMMARY:

The sacrament is an ordinance and a commandment designed by the Lord to help us remember His atoning sacrifice and the hope we have in Him of returning to live with our Father in Heaven. It is full of rich symbolism and offers an opportunity to renew our baptismal covenants, which also incorporate the same symbols. The bread represents the Savior's body, which was ransomed for us on the cross and later resurrected in glory. The wine (water) causes our mind to reflect on the blood which was shed for our sins and by which we are atoned for our sins. By partaking of the sacrament each week at church we thoughtfully consider our baptismal covenants and remember that through Christ, we too, can overcome physical and spiritual death.

God ordained the Sabbath to be kept holy and declared it to be a day of rest from our labors. When we partake of the sacrament on the Sabbath, we are born again and can rest from our sins by accepting the Atonement in our lives. It is the Savior who truly gives us rest.

QUOTES:

"Worthy partakers of the sacrament are in harmony with the Lord and put themselves under covenant with Him to always remember His sacrifice for the sins of the world, to take upon them the name of Christ and to always remember Him, and to keep His commandments. The Savior covenants that we who do so shall have His spirit to be with us and that, if faithful to the end, we may inherit eternal life" (David B. Haight, "The Sacrament—and the Sacrifice," *Ensign*, Nov. 1989).

"When we partake of the sacrament with a sincere heart, with real intent, forsaking our sins, and renewing our commitment to God, the Lord provides a way whereby sins can be forgiven" (Vaughn J. Featherstone, "Sacrament Meeting and the Sacrament," *Ensign*, Sept. 2001, 23–25).

"As we worthily partake of the sacrament, we will sense those things we need to improve in and receive the help and determination to do so. No matter what our problems, the sacrament always gives hope" (John H. Groberg, "The Beauty and Importance of the Sacrament," *Ensign*, May 1989, 38–40).

"Reminding us weekly of our need to foster charity toward our fellow Saints, the sacrament can be a great force for unity in our congregations" (John S. Tanner, Tambuli, "Reflections on the Sacrament Prayers," *Ensign*, Apr. 1986, 7–11).

"When we witness our willingness to take upon us the name of Jesus Christ, we are signifying our commitment to do all that we can to achieve eternal life in the kingdom of our Father. We are expressing our candidacy—our determination to strive for—exaltation in the celestial kingdom" (Dallin H. Oaks, "Taking Upon Us the Name of Jesus Christ," *Ensign*, May 1985, 80–83).

"Observance of the Sabbath is not a restriction but a source of strength and protection" (D. Kelly Ogden, "Remember the Sabbath Day," *Ensign,* Apr. 1994, 46–51).

"Our observance of the Sabbath is an indication of the depth of our conversion and our willingness to keep sacred covenants" (Earl C. Tingey, "The Sabbath Day and Sunday Shopping," *Ensign,* May 1996, 10–12).

GOSPEL ART:

John the Baptist Baptizing Jesus—(208 KIT, 35 GAB)
Jesus Washing the Apostles' Feet—(226 KIT, 55 GAB)
Jesus Praying in Gethsemane—(227 KIT, 56 GAB)
The Crucifixion—(230 KIT, 57 GAB)
Jesus' Burial—(232 KIT, 58 GAB)
Mary and the Resurrected Lord—(233 KIT, 59 GAB)
Jesus Shows His Wounds—(234 KIT, 60 GAB)
Jesus at the Door—(237 KIT, 65 GAB)
The Resurrected Jesus Christ—(239 KIT, 66 GAB)
Jesus the Christ—(240 KIT, 1 GAB)
The Empty Tomb—(245 KIT)
Blessing the Sacrament—(603 KIT, 107 GAB)
Passing the Sacrament—(604 KIT, 108 GAB)
Alma Baptizes in the Waters of Mormon—(309 KIT, 76 GAB)

VIDEOS:

  "Partake of the Sacrament": http://www.lds.org/media-library/video/2012-08-2895-partake-of-the-sacrament?lang=eng

  "Sacredness of the Sacrament": http://www.lds.org/media-library/video/2012-06-1370-sacredness-of-the-sacrament?lang=eng

- "Partake of the Sacrament Worthily": http://www.lds.org/media-library/video/2012-06-2270-partake-of-sacrament-worthily?lang=eng
- "Jesus Teaches of Being Born Again": http://www.lds.org/media-library/video/2011-10-028-jesus-teaches-of-being-born-again?lang=eng

OBJECT LESSONS:

- Take a picture out of a frame so that all that remains is the glass in the frame. Put some dirt or stains on one side and show it to the class. Explain that sometimes we don't even realize how dirty we're getting from the world because it accumulates over time. Use a glass cleaner to clean away the dirt on the glass. Discuss how going to church and partaking of the sacrament helps us to become unspotted from the world and have clearer vision. Invite someone from the class to read Doctrine and Covenants 59:9 while standing behind the glass.

- Invite someone in the class to enjoy an ice cream sundae with you. Dish out some ice cream and comment on how excited everyone looks about the yummy treat. Now put on various toppings such as pepperoni, BBQ sauce, chopped onions and grated cheese. The class will probably express disgust. Ask them why they don't want those toppings. They'll probably say that they like those ingredients, but not on top of a sundae. Talk about how choosing activities appropriate for Sunday is the same: activities we do during the week aren't bad activities, but they just may not be appropriate for the Sabbath day.

- Display a battery-operated flashlight with a weak battery. Talk about how ineffective it is and explain that when our spiritual batteries are recharged every week after taking the sacrament that our eternal vision is brighter.

ARTICLES:

- ❧ L. Tom Perry, "As Now We Take the Sacrament," *Ensign*, May 2006.

- ❧ Dallin H. Oaks, "Sacrament Meeting and the Sacrament," *Ensign*, Nov. 2008.

- ❧ Russell M. Nelson, "Worshiping at Sacrament Meeting," *Ensign*, Aug. 2004.

- ❧ David B. Haight, "The Sacrament—and the Sacrifice," *Liahona*, Apr. 2007.

- ❧ David B. Haight, "Remembering the Savior's Atonement," *Ensign*, Apr. 1988.

- ❧ W. Mack Lawrence, "Sunday Worship Service," *Ensign*, May 1991.

CHALLENGE:

Using Mosiah 18 as a guide, write a list of all the covenants that are made at baptism. Evaluate how you are doing with all of them and choose one you can do better with this week.

SEMINARY SCRIPTURE MASTERY:

Mosiah 4:30
Alma 34:32–34
Helaman 5:12

Exodus 20:3–17
D&C 59:9–10

PREACH MY GOSPEL:

Pages 31–34, 48, 51–52, 58, 60–61, 64

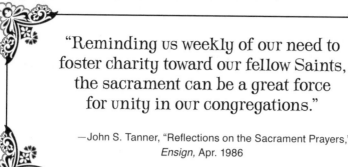

"Reminding us weekly of our need to foster charity toward our fellow Saints, the sacrament can be a great force for unity in our congregations."

—John S. Tanner, "Reflections on the Sacrament Prayers," *Ensign,* Apr. 1986

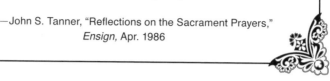

"Reminding us weekly of our need to foster charity toward our fellow Saints, the sacrament can be a great force for unity in our congregations."

—John S. Tanner, "Reflections on the Sacrament Prayers," *Ensign,* Apr. 1986

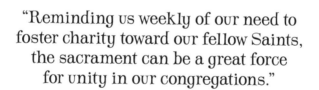

"Reminding us weekly of our need to foster charity toward our fellow Saints, the sacrament can be a great force for unity in our congregations."

—John S. Tanner, "Reflections on the Sacrament Prayers," *Ensign,* Apr. 1986

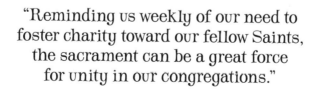

"Reminding us weekly of our need to foster charity toward our fellow Saints, the sacrament can be a great force for unity in our congregations."

—John S. Tanner, "Reflections on the Sacrament Prayers," *Ensign,* Apr. 1986

JOSEPH AND HYRUM SMITH, WITNESSES FOR JESUS CHRIST

Music

"An Angel Came to Joseph Smith"—Children's Songbook #86

"Come, Listen to a Prophet's Voice"—*Hymns* #21

"Joseph Smith's First Prayer"—*Hymns* #26

"Praise to the Man"—*Hymns* #27

"Truth Eternal"—*Hymns* #4

"We Thank Thee, O God, for a Prophet"—*Hymns* #19

SUMMARY:

Every member of the Church has to decide for herself what she believes about the Prophet Joseph, as it is the pivotal point of our religion. Every member can find that out by doing what he did, going to the Lord in earnest, sincere prayer. By studying and praying about the truthfulness of the Book of Mormon, the fruit of Joseph Smith's ministry, we can know if he truly was a prophet of the Lord sent to restore the fulness of the gospel in these latter days.

Through Joseph Smith, all of the keys and ordinances required for our salvation were restored to earth. Through Joseph's experiences and writings, we have a greater understanding of the nature of God and our relationship to Him. The Prophet Joseph was called to stand at the head of this dispensation and seal his testimony with his blood. Joseph's brother, Hyrum, was the second to seal his testimony with blood, fulfilling the Law of Witnesses. The young prophet gave his life for his testimony of the Savior; we should be willing to live our lives, testifying to others about what happened in that sacred grove of trees and in our own hearts.

QUOTES:

"Bonds and imprisonments and persecutions are no disgrace to the Saints. It is that that is common in all ages of the world since the days of Adam. . . . The same things produce the same effect in every age of the world. We only want the same patience, the same carefulness, the same guide, the same grace, the same faith in our Lord Jesus Christ. . . . What we do not learn by precept we may learn by experience. All these things are to make us wise and intelligent that we may be the happy recipients of the highest glory" (Hyrum Smith, Church Patriarch, 1841–1844, Letter to Mary Fielding Smith, ca. 1839, probably from Liberty Jail, Liberty, Missouri, Church Archives, The Church of Jesus Christ of Latter-day Saints, Salt Lake City, Utah; spelling, punctuation, and capitalization modernized).

"Through it all, Hyrum stood firm. He knew the course his life would take, and he consciously chose to follow it. To Joseph, Hyrum became companion, protector, provider, confidant, and eventually joined him as a martyr. Unjust persecution engulfed them throughout their lives. Although he was older, Hyrum recognized his brother's divine mantle" (M. Russell Ballard, "Hyrum Smith: 'Firm as the Pillars of Heaven,'" *Ensign*, Nov. 1995).

"No testimony is more significant to us in our time than the witness of Joseph Smith. He was the prophet chosen to restore the ancient Church of Christ in this, the last time when the gospel will be on the earth before the return of Jesus Christ. Like all the prophets who opened the work of God in their dispensations, Joseph was given especially clear and powerful prophetic experiences to prepare the world for the Savior's Second Coming" (Robert D. Hales, "Seeking to Know God, Our Heavenly Father, and His Son, Jesus Christ," *Ensign*, Nov. 2009, 30).

"The more I know of the Prophet Joseph, the more I love him, the more I yearn to follow his example, the more I appreciate what our Father in Heaven and His Son have done in restoring this gospel that is destined to fill the earth in these, the latter days" (Joseph B. Wirthlin, "Growing into the Priesthood," *Ensign*, Nov. 1999, 41).

"Like Joseph, we must search the scriptures and pray. For many, this means overcoming feelings of doubt and unworthiness, being humble, and learning to exercise faith" (Robert D. Hales, "Receiving a Testimony of the Restored Gospel of Jesus Christ," *Ensign*, Nov. 2003, 28–29).

GOSPEL ART:

The Bible and Book of Mormon: Two Witnesses—(326 KIT)
The Prophet Joseph Smith—(401 KIT, 122 GAB)
Joseph Smith Seeks Wisdom in the Bible—(402 KIT, 89 GAB)
The First Vision—(403 KIT, 90 GAB)
Moroni Appears to Joseph Smith in His Room—(404 KIT, 91 GAB)
Joseph Smith Receives the Gold Plates—(406 KIT)
John the Baptist Conferring the Aaronic Priesthood—(407 KIT, 93 GAB)
Melchizedek Priesthood Restoration—(408 KIT, 94 GAB)
Translating the Book of Mormon—(416 KIT, 92 GAB)
Elijah Restores the Power to Seal Families for Eternity—(417 KIT, 95 GAB)
Latter-day Prophets—(506–522 KIT, 122–137 GAB)

VIDEOS:

≈ "Come Out of the Darkness into the Light," James E. Faust: http://www.lds.org/media-library/video/ces-firesides?lang=eng &start=37&end=48#2002-09-05-come-out-of-the-darkness-into -the-light

- "A Search for Truth": http://lds.org/library/display/0,4945,6635 -1-4786-3,00.html

- "Joseph Smith: Prophet of the Restoration": http://lds.org /library/display/0,4945,6635-1-4786-3,00.html

- "Martyrdom of Joseph Smith": http://lds.org/library/display/0 ,4945,6635-1-4786-3,00.html

- "Joseph Smith Papers": http://lds.org/library/display/0,4945,66 35-1-4786-8,00.html

- "The Restoration": http://lds.org/media-library/video?lang=eng

- Joseph Smith Commemorative Broadcast: http://www.lds.org /media-library/video/other-videos?lang=eng#2004-10-01-joseph -smith-commemorative-broadcast

- "The Message of the Restoration": http://lds.org/media-library /video/mormon-messages?lang=eng#2009-02-04-the-message-of -the-restoration

OBJECT LESSONS:

- Ask someone to bend an old, thick stick. (They shouldn't be able to do it.) Now ask someone to bend a thin, young stick. The Lord needed someone teachable and flexible to restore His kingdom on earth; the Lord needed the young boy Joseph.

- Tell the class you're going to show pictures of different kinds of cars and that they're supposed to raise their hands when they see a car that represents the kind of person they are (sports car, truck, mini-van, race car, luxury sedan, taxi, etc.). Explain that all cars get old and eventually break down. Age, accidents, and everyday use will wear a car out. Sooner or later all cars are destined for the junk yard unless someone restores them. In some ways our lives are like the cars. Just as all cars break down, all people share a common problem that causes us to wear out and eventually die. Just as a car can't fix its own dent or flat tires, we can't fix the problem of death. The Savior keeps our cars running in good condition. He sends auto-mechanics (prophets) who know how to restore cars to their best state when they get old and rusty too.

- Invite someone to play a hymn or song on the piano, but tape down most of the piano keys. After the death of the early apostles, the authority was lost and the fulness of the gospel was not on earth. Explain that there are many wonderful churches on earth today that have some of the piano keys to enjoy, but that the Church of Jesus Christ allows us to enjoy the whole song as it was intended and the fulness of the gospel. Joseph Smith was an instrument in the Lord's hands.

ARTICLES:

- Dallin H. Oaks, "Joseph, the Man and the Prophet," *Ensign*, May 1996.
- Gordon B. Hinckley, "What Hath God Wrought through His Servant Joseph!" *Ensign*, Feb. 1997.
- Neal A. Maxwell, "The Wondrous Restoration," *Ensign*, Apr. 2003.
- Charles Didier, "The Message of the Restoration," *Ensign*, Nov. 2003.
- www.JosephSmithPapers.org

CHALLENGE:

Set a goal to read the Book of Mormon this year in your personal scripture study. Calculate how many pages a day you'll need to read to accomplish your objective.

SEMINARY SCRIPTURE MASTERY:

Alma 37:6–7   James 1:5–6
Helaman 5:12   Revelation 14:6–7
Isaiah 29:13–14   Joseph Smith History 1:15–20
Amos 3:7   D&C 1:37–38
2 Timothy 3:16–17   D&C 76:22–24

PREACH MY GOSPEL:

Pages 6–8, 36–37

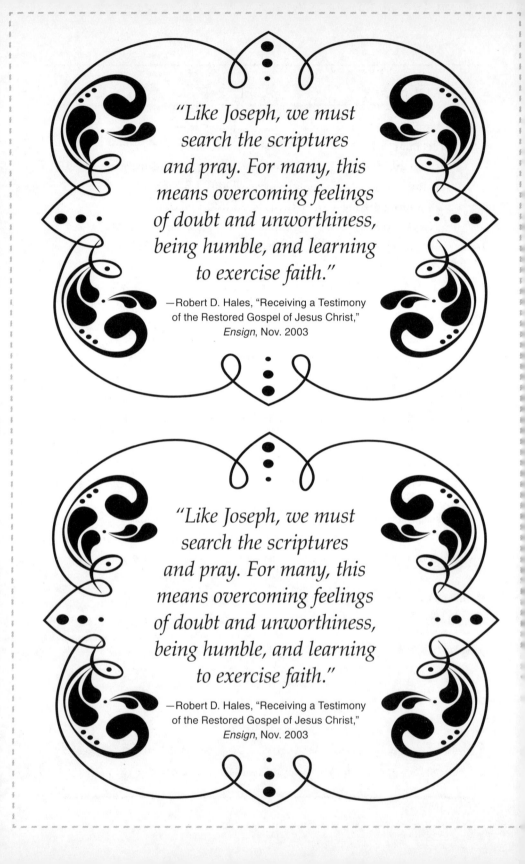

"Like Joseph, we must search the scriptures and pray. For many, this means overcoming feelings of doubt and unworthiness, being humble, and learning to exercise faith."

—Robert D. Hales, "Receiving a Testimony of the Restored Gospel of Jesus Christ," *Ensign*, Nov. 2003

"Like Joseph, we must search the scriptures and pray. For many, this means overcoming feelings of doubt and unworthiness, being humble, and learning to exercise faith."

—Robert D. Hales, "Receiving a Testimony of the Restored Gospel of Jesus Christ," *Ensign*, Nov. 2003

LESSON EIGHT

THE CHURCH AND KINGDOM OF GOD

Music

"The Glorious Gospel Light Has Shone"—*Hymns #283*
"Twas Witnessed in the Morning Sky"—*Hymns #12*
"High On the Mountain Top"—*Hymns #5*
"Let Earth's Inhabitants Rejoice"—*Hymns #53*
"Let Zion in Her Beauty Rise"—*Hymns #41*
"Hark, All Ye Nations!"—*Hymns #264*
"The Voice of God Again is Heard"—*Hymns #18*

SUMMARY:

After the Savior ascended into heaven, it wasn't long before His church and its ordinances and teachings were lost in their purity. Priesthood authority and correct doctrine were restored in 1830, when a prophet of God was again chosen. Jesus Christ leads His church today: The Church of Jesus Christ of Latter-day Saints. It offers the fulness of the gospel to the world and will never be destroyed again. Membership in the Lord's church will bring us happiness in mortality and salvation in the world to come.

A wise Heavenly Father designed His church to allow us to learn and grow by helping Him build His kingdom here on earth. He calls leaders to direct the work, and He expects us to support and sustain them. When we raise our hand in Church to sustain people in their callings, we are testifying that this is the Lord's church. When we use our hands and get to work to help those we sustain, we witness that we are willing to do our part too.

We are commanded to keep the commandments and teach them to others. When we do, our joy will be felt for eternity. The Lord entrusts us with this important work, and it is our privilege to be a part of it.

QUOTES:

"Today The Church of Jesus Christ of Latter-day Saints is extending the heralded message of the restoration of the gospel to every nation which permits us entrance through its borders. This is a fulfillment of the vision and revelation received by Daniel, the prophet. . . . This is the heaven-decreed destiny of this church and kingdom. . . . The Church will always stand for that which is honest, virtuous, true and praiseworthy" (Ezra Taft Benson, "May the Kingdom of God Go Forth," *Ensign*, May 1978).

"The Church is no bigger than a ward. . . . Everything needed for our redemption, save for the temple, is centered there—and temples now come ever closer to all of us" (Boyd K. Packer, "The Bishop and His Counselors," *Ensign*, May 1999, 57–63).

"We declare to the world that the fulness of the gospel of Jesus Christ has been restored to the earth" (L. Tom Perry, "The Message of the Restoration," *Ensign*, May 2007, 85–88).

"The dawn of the dispensation of the fulness of times rose upon the world. All of the good, the beautiful, the divine of all previous dispensations was restored in this most remarkable season" (Gordon B. Hinckley, "The Dawning of a Brighter Day," *Ensign*, May 2004, 83).

"We have long realized that the most important missionary tool is a good member of the Church" (Gordon B. Hinckley, "A Visit with Elder Gordon B. Hinckley about Missionary Work," *New Era*, June 1973).

GOSPEL ART:

Moses Calls Aaron to the Ministry—(108 KIT, 15 GAB)
Boy Samuel Called by the Lord—(111 KIT, 18 GAB)
Enoch and His People Are Taken Up to God—(120 KIT)

Lehi Prophesying to the People of Jerusalem—(300 KIT, 67 GAB)

King Benjamin Addresses His People—(307 KIT, 74 GAB)

Calling of the Fishermen—(209 KIT, 37 GAB)

Christ Ordaining the Apostles—(211 KIT, 38 GAB)

Jesus Washing the Apostles' Feet—(226 KIT, 55 GAB)

Christ with Three Nephite Disciples—(324 KIT)

Latter-day Prophets—(506 KIT, 122–27 GAB)

The Prophet Joseph Smith—(401 KIT, 122 GAB)

John the Baptist Conferring the Aaronic Priesthood—(407 KIT, 93 GAB)

Melchizedek Priesthood Restoration—(408 KIT, 94 GAB)

Sustaining Our Leaders—(610 KIT)

The Bishop—(611 KIT)

Jesus Christ—(240 KIT, 1 GAB)

Go Ye Therefore—(235 KIT, 61 GAB)

The Ascension of Jesus—(236 KIT, 62 GAB)

Jesus at the Door—(237 KIT, 65 GAB)

Brother Joseph—(400 KIT, 87 GAB)

The First Vision—(403 KIT, 90 GAB)

Dan Jones Preaching the Gospel in Wales—(100 GAB)

Young Man Being Baptized—(103 GAB)

Girl Being Baptized—(104 GAB)

Missionaries: Elders—(109 GAB)

Missionaries: Sisters—(110 GAB)

Daniel Interprets Nebuchadnezzar's Dream—(115 KIT, 24 GAB)

The Bible and Book of Mormon: Two Witnesses—(326 KIT)

Apostle Orson Hyde Dedicates the Holy Land—(419 KIT)

Pioneers Arrive by Ship in San Francisco Bay—(421 KIT)

Kirtland Temple—(500 KIT, 117 GAB)

Nauvoo Illinois Temple—(501 KIT, 118 GAB)

Salt Lake Temple—(502 KIT, 119 GAB)

VIDEOS:

- ❧ "Apostasy": http://www.lds.org/media-library/video/2009-04-044-apostasy-jan?lang=eng

- ❧ "Testimonies of the Apostles": http://lds.org/media-library/video/prophets-and-apostles-speak-today?lang=eng

- ❧ "After the New Testament": http://www.lds.org/media-library/video/2010-11-68-after-the-new-testament?lang=eng

- ❧ "As We Meet Together Again," Pres. Thomas S. Monson: http://www.lds.org/media-library/video/general-conference-october-2010?lang=eng&start=13&end=24

- ❧ "Church Growth by Stake": http://lds.org/library/display/0,4945,6635-1-4786-7,00.html

- ❧ "Why Mormons Send Missionaries Around the World": http://lds.org/media-library/video/our-faith?lang=eng&start=13&end=24

- ❧ "Congregational Service": http://lds.org/media-library/video/other-videos?lang=eng

OBJECT LESSON:

- ❧ Pass out gum to the class and tell them to chew it for about 5 minutes to get all of the flavor out of it. Now ask the class to put it back into the wrapper and mold it into the original form. Many men have tried to recreate Christ's true church. Only with the Savior's help was Joseph Smith able to restore the Lord's church.

- ❧ Show the class some tarnished silver spoons. Talk about what the restoration was while you polish the silver. Discuss how the beauty was always there, but that no one could see it until it was restored.

- Tell the class that a coin represents ancient and modern prophets. Ask them which side of the coin is more important. Then ask if the two sides of the coin can be separated. Explain that both sides of the coin work together for the same purpose, just as all prophets throughout the ages have had the common goal of bringing their people to Jesus Christ. Whatever calling we are given, that is our goal too!

- Display a large basket of goodies on the table at the front of the class and begin to eat from it, expressing great delight. Ask the class to share why they love the gospel so much. Continue snacking and then explain that when we enjoy the blessings of the gospel without sharing it with others, it's like you're having a basket of goodies that you love and not sharing it with the class. Pass the basket around and invite everyone to join you in eating yummy treats. At the end of the lesson, ask the sisters how many of them didn't take a treat, ate it right away, or planned on saving it for later. Explain that doing missionary work is similar—even when we share the sweet gospel with others, some people will accept and embrace it, others won't at all, and others might but not after many years.

- Invite the sisters to share their conversion stories.

ARTICLES:

- Jeffrey R. Holland, "This, The Greatest of All Dispensations," *Ensign*, July 2007.
- Russell M. Nelson, "Thus Shall My Church Be Called," *Ensign*, May 1990.
- D. Todd Christofferson, "Come to Zion," *Ensign*, Nov. 2008.
- Henry B. Eyring, "The True and Living Church," *Ensign*, May 2008.

- M. Russell Ballard, "The Truth of God Shall Go Forth," *Ensign*, Nov. 2008.
- Gordon B. Hinckley, "God Is at the Helm," *Ensign*, May 1994.
- Jeffrey R. Holland, "My Words . . . Never Cease," *Ensign*, May 2008.

CHALLENGE:

Write a list of all the ways you could magnify your calling in the Church. Start doing some of those things today. If you don't have a calling, ask your Bishop to give you one so you can help build the kingdom of God where you live!

SEMINARY SCRIPTURE MASTERY:

Alma 37:6–7

Helaman 5:12

Moses 1:39

Moses 7:18

Exodus 20:3–17

Daniel 2:44–45

Matthew 16:15–19

John 3:5, Ephesians 4:11–14

2 Thessalonians 2:1–3

Revelation 14:6–7

Joseph Smith History 1:15–20

D&C 58:26–27

D&C 84:33–39

PREACH MY GOSPEL:

Page 163

"The dawn of the dispensation of the fulness of times rose upon the world. All of the good, the beautiful, the divine of all previous dispensations was restored in this most remarkable season."

—Gordon B. Hinckley, "The Dawning of a Brighter Day," *Ensign*, May 2004

"The dawn of the dispensation of the fulness of times rose upon the world. All of the good, the beautiful, the divine of all previous dispensations was restored in this most remarkable season."

—Gordon B. Hinckley, "The Dawning of a Brighter Day," *Ensign*, May 2004

"The dawn of the dispensation of the fulness of times rose upon the world. All of the good, the beautiful, the divine of all previous dispensations was restored in this most remarkable season."

—Gordon B. Hinckley, "The Dawning of a Brighter Day," *Ensign*, May 2004

WITNESSES OF THE BOOK OF MORMON

Music

"As I Search the Holy Scriptures"—*Hymns* #277
"Book of Mormon Stories"—Children's Songbook #168
"From Homes of Saints Glad Songs Arise"—*Hymns* #297
"The Books in the Book of Mormon"—Children's Songbook #119
"Search, Ponder, and Pray"—Children's Songbook #109
"Seek the Lord Early"—Children's Songbook #108

SUMMARY:

An earnest desire for truth can lead to a powerful experience when seeking within the sacred pages of scripture. The Lord has preserved in holy writ the information He knows will help us in mortality and lead us to Him. We can find more comfort and wisdom in the Book of Mormon than in all other books ever caused to be written. The Book of Mormon is a sacred record that contains the fulness of the gospel and testifies that Jesus Christ is the Redeemer of the world.

The Law of Witnesses was fulfilled by three men who gave testimony when they saw an angel and the gold plates while hearing God's voice. Eight other men also handled the plates with their own hands. Each setting was different, but both experiences left no doubt in the minds and hearts of the witnesses for the rest of their lives.

The words in the Book of Mormon come from a loving Heavenly Father who wants us to know what is required to enter into His presence. As parents, it is vital to our children's salvation that we not only introduce them to the Book of Mormon, but also show how to search the scriptures, understand them, ascertain their truthfulness, and apply the teachings to their lives. Each of us can be a witness of the Book of Mormon.

QUOTES:

"We each need to get our own testimony of the Book of Mormon through the Holy Ghost. Then our testimony, coupled with the Book of Mormon, should be shared with others so that they, too, can know through the Holy Ghost of its truthfulness" (Ezra Taft Benson, "The Book of Mormon and the Doctrine of Covenants," *Ensign*, May 1987).

"Through reading the scriptures, we can gain the assurance of the Spirit that that which we read has come of God for the enlightenment, blessing, and joy of His children" (Gordon B. Hinckley, "Feasting Upon the Scriptures," *Ensign*, Dec. 1985, 42–45).

"The holy scriptures are like letters from home telling us how we can draw near to our Father in Heaven" (Ardeth G. Kapp, "The Holy Scriptures: Letters from Home," *Ensign*, Nov. 1985, 93–95).

"Each of us, at some time in our lives, must discover the Book of Mormon for ourselves—and not just discover it once, but rediscover it again and again" (Spencer W. Kimball, "How Rare a Possession—the Scriptures!" *Ensign*, Sept. 1976, 2–5).

"As a person studies the words of the Lord and obeys them, he or she draws closer to the Savior and obtains a greater desire to live a righteous life" (Merrill J. Bateman, "Coming Unto Christ by Searching the Scriptures," *Ensign*, Nov. 1992, 27–28).

GOSPEL ART:

Mormon Abridging the Plates—(306 KIT)
Moroni Hides the Plates in the Hill Cumorah—(320 KIT, 86 GAB)
Christ Asks for the Records—(323 KIT)
The Gold Plates—(325 KIT)
The Bible and Book of Mormon: Two Witnesses—(326 KIT)

Joseph Smith Seeks Wisdom in the Bible—(402 KIT, 89 GAB)
Saving the Book of Commandments—(409 KIT)
Translating the Book of Mormon—(416 KIT)
Search the Scriptures—(617 KIT)

VIDEOS:

- "A Book with a Promise": http://mormon.org/videos?gclid=CNj Cl9fnsasCFZBb7AodCm04iA

- "For Our Day": http://lds.org/library/display/0,4945,6635-1 -4786-2,00.html

- "True and Living God": http://lds.org/library/display/0,4945 ,6635-1-4786-7,00.html

- "Book of Mormon Testimonies": http://lds.org/media-library /video/prophets-and-apostles-speak-today?lang=eng&start =25&end=36

- "Another Testament of Jesus Christ—Richard": http://lds.org/ media-library/video/truth-restored?lang=eng

- "The Scriptures and the Restoration": http://lds.org/media- library/video/ces-firesides?lang=eng#2003-11-05-the-scriptures -and-the-restoration

- "Scriptures—More Precious Than Gold and Sweeter Than Honey": http://lds.org/media-library/video/ces-firesides?lang =eng#2005-09-04-scriptures-more-precious-than-gold -and-sweeter-than-honey

OBJECT LESSONS:

- Hold up a lollipop or some other piece of candy that has a wrapper. Ask for a volunteer who likes candy. Invite the volunteer to put the candy in her mouth. When she starts to take off the wrapper, say "I didn't say you could take the wrapper off. I just said you could put it in your mouth." Have her put the candy in her mouth with the wrapper on and ask her how it tastes. Ask her how long she thinks it will take for her saliva to dissolve the wrapper before she can taste the candy. Point out that her saliva has the ability to dissolve the hard candy, but not the wrapper. Talk about how the scriptures are very much like the candy. Because the scriptures were written by the power of the Holy Ghost they can't be understood unless a person has the help of the Holy Ghost. The mind of man alone does not have the ability to "take off the wrapper." Elder Howard W. Hunter said, "There is nothing more helpful than prayer to open our understanding of the scriptures." Finally, invite the volunteer and the whole class to enjoy some candy (without the wrappers on).

- Bring a plate of cookies and ask for volunteers to demonstrate different styles of eating: abstain, sample, taste, snack, gorge, nibble, eat, and feast. Now compare those styles to how we study the scriptures, reminding the class that we should "feast upon the words of Christ."

- Show the class two pictures that seem very much alike but have a few differences. Have the class point out the differences. In order to align our life with the Lord's will we need to follow His example found in the scriptures and change our life to match His model for us.

- Show the class an old, rotten banana and ask for a volunteer to eat it. (No one will want to.) Ask the class why they don't think it will taste very good. Now hold up a good banana and ask why anyone would choose to eat this one. Explain that our lives are like fruit; people can tell what kind of people we are by the fruit we produce. Matthew 7:20 says, 'Wherefore by their fruits ye shall know them." Ask "What kind of fruit do you want to produce?" Then, explain, "You may be the only Book of Mormon people will ever 'read.' Live your lives so that others can tell you're a disciple of Christ and want to know more."

🙺 Ask a class member to play a hymn on the harmonica. (Pick someone who doesn't know how to play it.) When they explain that they can't do it, ask them how they could learn. The answer is to study a manual or learn from someone who can. The same applies to learning to be like Heavenly Father; we can learn about Him in the Book of Mormon and we can follow the Savior, who is like Him. Daily practice makes perfect!

ARTICLES:

🙺 Dallin H. Oaks, "Feasting on the Word," *Ensign*, Mar. 2003, 35–36.

🙺 Henry B. Eyring, "A Discussion on Scripture Study," *Ensign*, July 2005.

🙺 Ezra Taft Benson, "The Book of Mormon is the Word of God," *Ensign*, Jan. 1988.

🙺 Ezra Taft Benson, "The Book of Mormon and the Doctrine and Covenants," *Ensign*, May 1987.

🙺 Daniel C. Peterson, "Mounting Evidence for the Book of Mormon," *Ensign*, Jan. 2000.

🙺 L. Tom Perry, "Give Heed Unto the Word of the Lord," *Ensign*, 2000.

CHALLENGE:

Write your testimony in some copies of the Book of Mormon and share your witness with a non-member this week. Give the remaining copies to the missionaries to share with their investigators.

SEMINARY SCRIPTURE MASTERY:

Alma 37:6–7

2 Thessalonians 2:1–3

Moroni 10:4–5

2 Timothy 3:16–17

Isaiah 29:13–14

James 1:5–6

Ezekiel 37:15–17

Revelation 14:6–7

John 10:16

PREACH MY GOSPEL:

Pages 7, 38–39, 103–4, 110–11, 105–8, 130

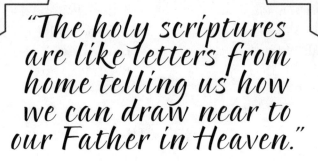

"The holy scriptures
are like letters from
home telling us how
we can draw near to
our Father in Heaven."

—Ardeth G. Kapp, "The Holy Scriptures:
Letters from Home," *Ensign,* Nov. 1985

"The holy scriptures
are like letters from
home telling us how
we can draw near to
our Father in Heaven."

—Ardeth G. Kapp, "The Holy Scriptures:
Letters from Home," *Ensign,* Nov. 1985

LESSON TEN

OUR SEARCH FOR TRUTH

Music

"Father in Heaven, We Do Believe"—*Hymns* #180
"I Believe in Christ,"—*Hymns* #134
"Guide Me to Thee"—*Hymns* #101
"Lead Me into Life Eternal"—*Hymns* #45
"Teach Me to Walk in the Light"—*Hymns* #304
"The Light Divine"—*Hymns* #305

SUMMARY:

As members of the Church, we should be an ever learning people–not just a learned people. There are so many fascinating things to learn about. Our spiritual education is even more important than our worldly academic pursuits. As we increase our education and learning, we should measure what we learn with the standards of gospel truth and through the guidance of the Holy Ghost.

The gospel of Jesus Christ isn't about learning interesting scriptural facts or debating doctrine, but rather, it is about applying those principles to our behavior and becoming Christ-like in all that we say and do. Religion isn't just something we believe, but truly the blueprint for how we live our daily lives.

As we increase our faith by studying the scriptures and testing the principles of the gospel in our lives, the Lord will increase our light and understanding. As members of the Church, we are expected to learn the gospel, live it, and share it. It should be our goal to progress from *knowing* to *doing* to *becoming*. Heavenly Father cares more about who we are than what we know.

QUOTES:

"God has created man with a mind capable of instruction, and a faculty which may be enlarged in proportion to the heed and diligence given to the light communicated from heaven to the intellect; and . . . the nearer man approaches perfection, the clearer are his views, and the greater his enjoyments, till he has overcome the evils of his life and lost every desire for sin; and like the ancients, arrives at that point of faith where he is wrapped in the power and glory of his Maker, and is caught up to dwell with Him" (Joseph Smith, *History of the Church*, 2:8).

"The thing about truth is that it exists beyond belief. It is true even if nobody believes it. . . . However, there is indeed such a thing as absolute truth—unassailable, unchangeable truth. . . . This truth is different from belief. It is different from hope. Absolute truth is not dependent upon public opinion or popularity. . . . Yes, our world is full of confusion. But eventually all of our questions will be answered. All of our doubts will be replaced by certainty. And that is because there is one source of truth that is complete, correct, and incorruptible. That source is our infinitely wise and all-knowing Heavenly Father. He knows truth as it was, as it is, and as it yet will be" (Dieter F. Uchtdorf, "What is Truth," CES Devotional, 2013).

"The Holy Ghost is a certain and safe guide to assist all mortals who seek God as they navigate the often troubling waters of confusion and contradiction. . . . Yes, your loving Father in Heaven would never leave you alone in this mortality to wander in the dark. You need not be deceived. You can overcome the darkness of this world and discover divine truth" (Dieter F. Uchtdorf, "What is Truth," CES Devotional, 2013).

"As disciples of the Savior, we are not merely striving to know more; rather, we need to consistently do more of what we know is right and become better. We should remember that bearing a heartfelt testimony is only a beginning. We need to bear testimony, we need to mean it, and most importantly we need consistently to live it. We need to both declare and live our testimonies" (David A. Bednar, "More Diligent and Concerned at Home," *Ensign*, Nov. 2009, 19).

"Reading and studying the scriptures make us conscious of the many conditional promises made by the Lord to encourage obedience and righteous living" (Howard W. Hunter, "Commitment to God," *Ensign*, Nov. 1982, 57–58).

"The word of the Lord in the scriptures is like a lamp to guide our feet, and revelation is like a mighty force that increases the lamp's illumination manyfold" (Dallin H. Oaks, "Feasting on the Word," *Ensign*, Mar. 2003).

"Personal revelation is the way we know for ourselves the most important truths of our existence" (Dallin H. Oaks, "Revelation," *New Era*, Sept. 1982).

GOSPEL ART:

Adam and Eve Teaching Their Children—(5 GAB)
Jesus at the Door—(237 KIT, 65 GAB)
Boy Jesus in the Temple—(205 KIT, 34 GAB)
Joseph Smith Seeks Wisdom in the Bible—(402 KIT, 89 GAB)
Young Boy Praying—(605 KIT, 111 GAB)
Family Prayer—(606 KIT, 112 GAB)
Search the Scriptures—(617 KIT)
Jesus the Christ—(240 KIT, 65 and 66 GAB)
Passing the Sacrament—(604 KIT, 108 GAB)
The Articles of Faith—(618 KIT)
My Gospel Standards—(619 KIT)

VIDEOS:

- ❧ "The Most Important Things to Learn": http://www.lds.org /media-library/video/2012-07-1040-the-most-important-things -to-learn?lang=eng

- ❧ "Seek Learning By Faith": http://www.lds.org/media-library /video/2013-02-2040-133-seek-learning-by-faith?lang=eng

- ❧ "You Know Enough": www.lds.org/ldsorg/v/index.jsp?vgnextoid =bd163ca6e9aa3210VgnVCM1000003a94610aRCRD&locale=0

- ❧ "Spiritual Vertigo": http://mormonchannel.org/video?v=1101 413009001

- ❧ "Seek the Guidance of the Spirit": http://lds.org/service/serving -in-the-church/relief-society/leader-resources/sunday-relief-society -meetings/seek-guidance-of-the-spirit?lang=eng&query=revelation +(collection%3a"media")

OBJECT LESSONS:

- ❧ Teach the sisters about the BYU Idaho Pathway program that allows any student over the age of 18 to earn a degree online. There may be many sisters in your ward who began a college degree, yet never finished. Invite students who may have participated in the Pathway program to share their personal experiences. You can learn more about it at: www.byui.edu/online/pathway.

- ❧ Show everyone a picture of the solar system and explain that the sun is the center of our solar system with all of the planets revolving around it. Discuss how rotation and revolution ensure our planet's constant light and heat. Explain that the Savior offers us the spiritual light (truth) and warmth (love) that we need to guide us. Point out that to enjoy the full benefits of this, we must keep Him as the center of our lives. We can demonstrate His importance in our lives by revolving our lives around Him. Discuss how this can be done (regular prayers, scripture study, meeting attendance, and daily actions).

꙾ Shine a spotlight on someone. Now ask her to move one step away. Point out that she may still have a little bit of light on her but not as much as before. Now ask her to move five steps away and show that she no longer has any light on her. The light is Jesus Christ. He is not the one who moves. It only takes one step away from the Lord to reduce His light on us. When we step away from the gospel in search of worldly knowledge, we can't see truth in its full light. To continue to receive the Lord's illumination in our lives, we can't move . . . we have to stay close to Him and keep the commandments.

꙾ Encourage the class to create their own object lessons by sharing things they have learned in school or life and turning them into spiritual lessons learned.

ARTICLES:

꙾ Elder David A. Bednar, "Learning to Love Learning," *Ensign*, Feb. 2010.

꙾ Gordon B. Hinckley, "Words of the Prophet: Seek Learning," *New Era*, Sept. 2007.

꙾ Dallin H. Oaks, "Learning and Latter-day Saints," *Liahona*, Apr. 2009.

꙾ Howard W. Hunter, "Commitment to God," *Ensign*, Nov. 1982, 57–58.

꙾ Bernard P. Brockbank, "Knowing God," *Ensign*, July 1972, 121–23.

CHALLENGE:

Sign up to be a Speaking Partner for an international student in the BYU–Idaho Pathway Program at www.byui.edu/online/speaking-partners. International online students need to practice speaking English and will use their weekly course material to direct the conversation with a volunteer via Skype for 30 minutes once a week. Speaking Partners need only commit to one semester at a time. You will love meeting these wonderful students from around the world.

SEMINARY SCRIPTURE MASTERY:

1 Nephi 19:23

2 Nephi 9:28–29

2 Nephi 32:3

2 Nephi 32:8–9

Helaman 5:12

Moroni 7:16–17

Moroni 10:4–5

Moses 7:18

John 7:17

2 Timothy 3:16–17

James 1:5–6

D&C 130:18–19

D&C 130:20–21

PREACH MY GOSPEL:

Page 21

"Reading and studying the scriptures make us conscious of the many conditional promises made by the Lord to encourage obedience and righteous living."

—Howard W. Hunter, "Commitment to God," *Ensign*, Nov. 1982, 57–58

"Reading and studying the scriptures make us conscious of the many conditional promises made by the Lord to encourage obedience and righteous living."

—Howard W. Hunter, "Commitment to God," *Ensign*, Nov. 1982, 57–58

HONORING THE PRIESTHOOD KEYS RESTORED THROUGH JOSEPH SMITH

Music

"Ye Elders of Israel"—*Hymns* #319
"The Priesthood of Our Lord"—*Hymns* #320
"Come, All Ye Sons of God"—*Hymns* #322
"Rise Up, O Men of God"—*Hymns* #324
"See the Mighty Priesthood Gathered"—*Hymns* #325
"The Priesthood Is Restored"—Children's Songbook #89

SUMMARY:

The priesthood is the power and authority of God given to righteous men to enable them to act in God's name for the salvation of the human family. Earthly ordinances, such as baptism, confirmation, administration of the sacrament, and temple sealing ordinances, need to be performed by the correct priesthood authority in order to be valid in the eyes of the Lord. The same power Christ used to create the earth is given to worthy men.

When the Savior established His church during His earthly ministry, He chose humble men to serve as His apostles. When He needed to restore His gospel in latter-days, He did it through a humble young boy. The Lord always looks for the humble in spirit to bear His priesthood and to lead His church. Each of the Twelve Apostles holds all of the priesthood keys on earth; however, only the president of the Church can exercise them in full on behalf of the Church. The united voice of those who hold the keys of the kingdom of God will always guide us to spiritual safety.

Good men and women of all religions are blessed, but without correct divine authority, they cannot receive saving ordinances and attain a celestial glory. As women, we can inspire priesthood holders around us to honor their priesthood power and use it to bless others' lives.

QUOTES:

"Priesthood is to be used for the benefit of the entire human family, for the upbuilding of men, women, and children alike. There is indeed no privileged class or sex within the true Church of Christ. . . . Men have their work to do and their powers to exercise for the benefit of all the members of the Church. So with woman: Her special gifts are to be exercised for the benefit and uplift of the race" (John A. Widtsoe, comp., *Priesthood and Church Government*, rev. ed. [1954], 92–93).

"When one becomes a holder of the priesthood, he becomes an agent of the Lord. He should think of his calling as though he were on the Lord's errand, for indeed he is" (Harold B. Lee, "To Learn, to Do, to Be," *Ensign*, November 2008, 60–62, 67–68).

"The man holds the Priesthood, performs the priestly duties of the Church, but his wife enjoys with him every other privilege derived from the possession of the Priesthood. This is made clear, as an example, in the Temple service of the Church. The ordinances of the Temple are distinctly of Priesthood character, yet women have access to all of them, and the highest blessings of the Temple are conferred only upon a man and his wife jointly" (*Priesthood and Church Government* [1965], 83).

"I like to define the Priesthood in terms of service and I frequently call it the perfect plan of service. I do so because it seems to me that it is only through the utilization of the divine power conferred on men that they may ever hope to realize the full import and vitality of this endowment" (Stephen L. Richards, "To Learn, to Do, to Be," *Ensign*, Nov. 2008, 60–62, 67–68).

"Caring for others is the very essence of priesthood responsibility. It is the power to bless, to heal, and to administer the saving ordinances of the gospel" (James E. Faust, "Power of the Priesthood," *Ensign*, May 1997, 41–43).

"When we consider how few men who have lived on earth have received the priesthood and how Jesus Christ has empowered those individuals to act in His name, we should feel deeply humble and profoundly grateful for the priesthood we hold." (Richard G. Scott, "Honor the Priesthood and Use It Well," *Ensign*, Nov. 2008, 44–47).

"With the priesthood, nothing is impossible in carrying forward the work of the kingdom of God. . . . It is the only power on the earth that reaches beyond the veil of death" (Gordon B. Hinckley, "Priesthood Restoration," *Ensign*, Oct. 1988, 69–72).

GOSPEL ART:

Moses Calls Aaron to the Ministry—(108 KIT, 15 GAB)
Jacob Blessing His Sons—(122 KIT, 12 GAB)
Calling of the Fishermen—(209 KIT, 37 GAB)
Christ Ordaining the Apostles—(211 KIT, 38 GAB)
Christ Healing a Blind Man—(213 KIT)
Jesus Blessing Jairus's Daughter—(215 KIT, 41 GAB)
Jesus Washing the Apostles' Feet—(226 KIT, 55 GAB)
Christ With the Three Disciples—(324 KIT)
John the Baptist Conferring the Aaronic Priesthood—(407 KIT, 93 GAB)
Melchizedek Priesthood Restoration—(408 KIT, 94 GAB)
Baptism—(601 KIT, 103 GAB)
The Gift of the Holy Ghost—(602 KIT, 105 GAB)
Blessing the Sacrament—(603 KIT, 107 GAB)
Passing the Sacrament—(604 KIT, 108 GAB)

The Bishop—(611 KIT)

Missionaries Teach the Gospel of Jesus Christ—(612 KIT, 109 and 110 GAP)

Administering to the Sick—(613 KIT)

Home Teaching—(614 KIT)

VIDEOS:

- ❧ "Blessings of the Priesthood": http://mormon.org/videos?gclid =CNjCl9fnsasCFZBb7AodCm04iA

- ❧ "Elder Perry on Priesthood" (4 parts): http://lds.org/media -library/video/prophets-and-apostles-speak-today?lang=eng &start=13&end=24

- ❧ "Restoration of the Priesthood": http://lds.org/media-library /video/our-faith?lang=eng

- ❧ "Willing and Worthy to Serve": http://www.lds.org/media -library/video/2012-04-3060-president-thomas-s-monson ?lang=eng

OBJECT LESSONS:

- ❧ Take a "Master" lock and attach a sign to it that says "Eternal Life." The only way to get "Eternal Life" is if you unlock the lock. Have several keys that you can give to a class member and let her take one while passing the rest to the person next to her. Have them continue taking a key and passing them on. Discuss how the keys of the priesthood are passed from one individual to another worthy individual. Once the keys are passed, ask a person without a key to unlock the lock to gain eternal life. She will not be able to because she doesn't have a key. Then give the lock to the person that has the correct key. Discuss how ordinances need to be performed by the correct authority or else they will not be able to open the lock of eternal life.

ɜ➤ Ask someone in the class to hold an umbrella and keep someone in the class dry from the pretend rain that is falling. Note that the umbrella only needs to be held by one person, but both people are kept dry from the rain. So it is with the priesthood; while men can hold the priesthood, it is meant to be used to bless everyone and keep us all protected from the storms of earthly life.

ɜ➤ Show a credit card and ask, "What is this used for? What do you have to do to obtain it? Is it possible to have a credit card that doesn't work?" Now talk about the priesthood and ask the same three questions, comparing our "credit" to our personal worthiness to use the priesthood.

ARTICLES:

ɜ➤ Thomas S. Monson, "Our Sacred Priesthood Trust," *Liahona*, May 2006.

ɜ➤ Dallin H. Oaks, "Priesthood Blessings," *Ensign*, May 1987.

ɜ➤ Thomas S. Monson, "The Priesthood—A Sacred Gift," *Ensign*, May 2007.

ɜ➤ Russell M. Nelson, "Honoring the Priesthood," *Ensign*, May 1993.

ɜ➤ Henry B. Eyring, "God Helps the Faithful Priesthood Holder," *Liahona*, Nov. 2007.

ɜ➤ Richard G. Scott, "Honor the Priesthood and Use It Well," *Ensign*, Nov. 2008.

ɜ➤ Claudio R. M. Costa, "Priesthood Responsibilities," *Ensign*, May 2009.

ɜ➤ Thomas S. Monson, "True To Our Priesthood Trust," *Ensign*, Nov. 2006.

- James E. Faust, "A Royal Priesthood," *Ensign*, May 2006.
- Russell M. Nelson, "Personal Priesthood Responsibility," *Ensign*, Nov. 2003.

CHALLENGE:

Volunteer to drive a Deacon to do his Fast Offering route on the next Fast Sunday.

SEMINARY SCRIPTURE MASTERY:

Abraham 3:22–23
Matthew 16:15–19
Ephesians 4:11–14
Hebrews 5:4

D&C 1:37–38
D&C 84:33–39
D&C 121:34–36
D&C 130:20–21

PREACH MY GOSPEL:

Pages 32, 37, 83–84, 218

"With the priesthood, nothing is impossible in carrying forward the work of the kingdom of God. . . . It is the only power on the earth that reaches beyond the veil of death."

—Gordon B. Hinckley, "Priesthood Restoration," *Ensign*, Oct. 1988

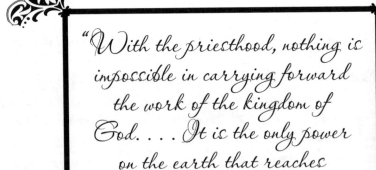

"With the priesthood, nothing is impossible in carrying forward the work of the kingdom of God. . . . It is the only power on the earth that reaches beyond the veil of death."

—Gordon B. Hinckley, "Priesthood Restoration," *Ensign*, Oct. 1988

THE OATH AND COVENANT OF THE PRIESTHOOD

Music

"Ye Elders of Israel"—*Hymns* #319

"The Priesthood of Our Lord"—*Hymns* #320

"Come, All Ye Sons of God"—*Hymns* #322

"Rise Up, O Men of God"—*Hymns* #323

"See the Mighty Priesthood"—*Hymns* #325

SUMMARY:

The priesthood is the power of God, given to righteous men to act for Him and administer His work on the earth. The Melchizedek Priesthood is conferred on worthy men and includes the offices of elder, high priest, patriarch, seventy, and apostle. The lesser priesthood, the Aaronic Priesthood, includes the offices of deacon, teacher, priest, and bishop. Boys and men are ordained to an office of the priesthood and placed in a quorum, performing specific duties and giving service to others.

The Lord takes oaths very seriously, so men should have a clear understanding of the oath and covenant of the priesthood they make when they are ordained to various offices in the priesthood, as outlined in Doctrine and Covenants 84. The promise of exaltation that is extended to worthy priesthood holders who are true and faithful to the oath and covenant of the priesthood is shared by their worthy wives.

QUOTES:

"Of all the holy agreements . . . few, if any, would transcend in importance the oath and covenant of the priesthood. It is certainly one of the most sacred agreements, for it involves the sharing of heavenly powers and man's upward reaching toward eternal goals" (Carlos E. Asay, "The Oath and Covenant of the Priesthood," *Ensign*, Nov. 1985).

"When ordained to an office in the priesthood, you are granted authority. But power comes from exercising that authority in righteousness" (Russell M. Nelson, "Personal Priesthood Responsibility," *Ensign*, Nov. 2003, 44–47).

"With the priesthood, nothing is impossible in carrying forward the work of the kingdom of God. . . . It is the only power on the earth that reaches beyond the veil of death" (Gordon B. Hinckley, "Priesthood Restoration," *Ensign*, Oct. 1988, 69–72).

"The priesthood of God gives light to His children in this dark and troubled world" (Robert D. Hales, "Blessings of the Priesthood," *Ensign*, Nov. 1995, 32–34).

"While the power of the priesthood is unlimited, our individual power in the priesthood is limited by our degree of righteousness or purity" (John H. Groberg, "Priesthood Power," *Ensign*, May 2001, 43–44).

GOSPEL ART:

Moses Calls Aaron to the Ministry—(108 KIT, 15 GAB)
Jacob Blessing His Sons—(122 KIT, 12 GAB)
Calling of the Fishermen—(209 KIT, 37 GAB)
Christ Ordaining the Apostles—(211 KIT, 38 GAB)
Christ Healing a Blind Man—(213 KIT)
Jesus Blessing Jairus's Daughter—(215 KIT, 41 GAB)
Jesus Washing the Apostles' Feet—(226 KIT, 55 GAB)
Christ With the Three Disciples—(324 KIT)

John the Baptist Conferring the Aaronic Priesthood—(407 KIT, 93 GAB)

Melchizedek Priesthood Restoration—(408 KIT, 94 GAB)

Baptism—(601 KIT, 103 GAB)

The Gift of the Holy Ghost—(602 KIT, 105 GAB)

Blessing the Sacrament—(603 KIT, 107 GAB)

Passing the Sacrament—(604 KIT, 108 GAB)

The Bishop—(611 KIT)

Missionaries Teach the Gospel of Jesus Christ—(612 KIT, 109 and 110 GAP)

Administering to the Sick—(613 KIT)

Home Teaching—(614 KIT)

VIDEOS:

- "Let Every Man Learn His Duty: Aaronic Priesthood":
  http://www.lds.org/media-library/video/2010-12-06-let-every-man
  -learn-his-duty-aaronic-priesthood?lang=eng

- "Becoming a Priesthood Man: Priesthood Duty":
  http://www.lds.org/media-library/video/2010-12-08-becoming
  -a-priesthood-man-priesthood-duty?lang=eng

- "Priesthood and Priesthood Keys—We Are Brothers":
  http://www.lds.org/media-library/video/2012-10-006-priesthood
  -and-priesthood-keys-we-are-brothers?lang=eng

- "Be Valiant in Courage, Strength, and Activity":
  http://www.lds.org/media-library/video/2012-10-3020-bishop
  -gary-e-stevenson?lang=eng

OBJECT LESSONS:

~ Show the class a gyroscope. It's not just a toy, but a scientific instrument. To make it work, you start it spinning and pull the string. If you put it on a tiny surface, it will still spin and stay upright. In fact, whatever the position it's placed in, it will continue to spin. The gyroscope principle is used in a special type of compass used on a ship because the movement won't affect it. There are many things that can knock us off course in life, but if we follow the leadership of the priesthood, our direction will always be right.

~ Help the sisters memorize a part of the Oath and Covenant of the Priesthood in Doctrine and Covenants 84. Try some of the memorizing techniques at www.wikihow.com/Memorize .

~ Invite someone from each priesthood quorum to share with the sisters what their responsibilities are in serving as a deacon, teacher, priest, elder, and high priest. You might also invite a patriarch or seventy if they're available.

ARTICLES:

~ Henry B. Eyring, "Faith and the Oath and Covenant of the Priesthood," *Ensign*, May 2008.

~ Carlos E. Asay, "The Oath and Covenant of the Priesthood," *Ensign*, Nov. 1985.

~ Thomas S. Monson, "Our Sacred Priesthood Trust," *Ensign*, May 2006.

~ Dallin H. Oaks, "Priesthood Blessings," *Ensign*, May 1987.

~ Thomas S. Monson, "The Priesthood—A Sacred Gift," *Ensign*, May 2007.

~ Russell M. Nelson, "Honoring the Priesthood," *Ensign*, May 1993.

🕊 Thomas S. Monson, "True To Our Priesthood Trust," *Ensign*, Nov. 2006.

CHALLENGE:

Help a priesthood holder memorize the Oath and Covenant of the priesthood outlined in Doctrine and Covenants 84.

SEMINARY SCRIPTURE MASTERY:

Abraham 3:22–23   D&C 1:37–38
Matthew 16:15–19   D&C 84:33–39
Ephesians 4:11–14   D&C 121:34–36
Hebrews 5:4   D&C 130:20–21

PREACH MY GOSPEL:

Pages 32, 37, 83–84, 218

"While the power of the priesthood is unlimited, our individual power in the priesthood is limited by our degree of righteousness or purity."

—John H. Groberg, "Priesthood Power,"
Ensign, May 2001

"While the power of the priesthood is unlimited, our individual power in the priesthood is limited by our degree of righteousness or purity."

—John H. Groberg, "Priesthood Power,"
Ensign, May 2001

"While the power of the priesthood is unlimited, our individual power in the priesthood is limited by our degree of righteousness or purity."

—John H. Groberg, "Priesthood Power,"
Ensign, May 2001

LESSON THIRTEEN

BAPTISM

"Lord, Accept Into Thy Kingdom"—*Hymns* #236
"Come, Follow Me"—*Hymns* #116
"Father in Heaven, We Do Believe"—*Hymns* #180
"Jesus, Mighty King in Zion"—*Hymns* #234
"When I Am Baptized"—Children's Songbook #103

SUMMARY:

To demonstrate our true repentance, we must follow the Savior and be baptized. Baptism by immersion for the remission of sins is an essential requirement for entry into the celestial kingdom. When we humble ourselves and are baptized we receive the Holy Ghost and are admitted into the Lord's church. Baptism by water is a symbol of spiritual cleansing, representing birth, death, and resurrection. The Gift of the Holy Ghost is the symbol of spiritual cleansing by fire.

Children under the age of eight do not need baptism yet, because they are redeemed through the Atonement of Jesus Christ. Anyone eight years old or older who is baptized into the Church of Jesus Christ of Latter-day Saints takes upon himself the name of Christ and enters into a covenant with God. The baptismal covenant includes a promise to keep the commandments, serve God, stand as His witness, bear each other's burdens, and come unto the fold of God. The guidance of the Holy Ghost can help us keep those promises each day.

QUOTES:

"[Baptism] is a sign and a commandment which God has set for man to enter into His kingdom. Those who seek to enter in any other way will seek in vain; for God will not receive them, neither will the angels acknowledge their works as accepted, for they have not obeyed the ordinances, nor attended to the signs which God ordained for the salvation of man, to prepare him for, and give him a title to, a celestial glory" (Joseph Smith, *History of the Church*, 4:554).

"Baptism is a holy ordinance preparatory to the reception of the Holy Ghost; it is the channel and key by which the Holy Ghost will be administered. The Gift of the Holy Ghost by the laying on of hands, cannot be received through the medium of any other principle than the principle of righteousness" (*Teachings: Joseph Smith*, 95–96).

"Baptism cleanses the soul from sin and prepares a person to lead a better, more perfect life in the future" (Theodore M. Burton, "To Be Born Again," *Ensign*, Sept. 1985, 66–70).

"Faith and repentance, baptism and bestowal of the Holy Ghost constitute the heart of the gospel of Jesus Christ, being the essential requirements for entry into the celestial kingdom" (Bruce D. Porter, "The First Principles and Ordinances of the Gospel," *Ensign*, Oct. 2000, 8–15).

"The full benefit of forgiveness of sin through the Savior's Atonement begins with repentance and baptism and then expands upon receiving the Holy Ghost" (James E. Faust, "Born Again," *Ensign*, May 2001, 54–55).

"Baptism is the beginning of a new life for each one of us, a life of purpose" (Dwan J. Young, "Keeping the Covenants We Make at Baptism," *Ensign*, Nov. 1984, 94–95).

GOSPEL ART:

John the Baptist Baptizing Jesus—(208 KIT, 35 GAB)
Alma Baptizes in the Waters of Mormon—(309 KIT, 76 GAB)
Baptism—(601 KIT, 103 and 104 GAB)

The Gift of the Holy Ghost—(602 KIT, 105 GAB)
Young Man Being Baptized—(103 GAB)
Girl Being Baptized—(104 GAB)
Temple Baptismal Font—(121 GAB)

VIDEOS:

- Share some of the many inspiring conversion stories at: https://www.lds.org/media-library/video/truth-restored?lang =eng&start=13&end=24

- "The Baptism of Jesus": http://www.lds.org/bible-videos/videos /the-baptism-of-jesus?lang=eng

- "Jesus Teaches of Being Born Again": http://www.lds.org/media -library/video/2011-10-028-jesus-teaches-of-being-born-again?lang =eng

- "Baptism for Dead": http://www.lds.org/media-library/video /2012-06-2320-baptism-for-dead?lang=eng

OBJECT LESSONS:

- Ask the class if they would like some gum. When they express interest, pass out a plate with pieces of gum that have already been chewed, as well as pieces of gum still wrapped up "clean and pure." Act surprised when no one chooses the already chewed gum. Talk about how baptism washes us clean and makes us appear more presentable to the Lord.

- Show a hard boiled egg and explain that it represents how we all come to earth: pure and unblemished. Draw all over the shell with crayons while you talk about the sins we make in life that tarnish us. (Don't use markers because they can bleed through the shell and ruin the visual effect!) Carefully peel the egg to show how baptism allows us to shed our worldly self and become pure and unblemished again.

ARTICLES:

- Robert D. Hales, "The Covenant of Baptism: To Be In the Kingdom and Of the Kingdom," *Ensign*, Nov. 2000.
- D. Todd Christofferson, "Born Again," *Ensign*, May 2008.
- James E. Faust, "Born Again," *Ensign*, May 2001.
- David E. Sorensen, "Why Baptism Is Not Enough," *Ensign*, Apr. 1999.
- Theodore M. Burton, "To Be Born Again," *Ensign*, Sept. 1985.
- Carol B. Thomas, "Spiritual Power of Our Baptism," *Ensign*, May 1999.
- Robert D. Hales, "The Covenant of Baptism: To Be In the Kingdom and Of the Kingdom," *Ensign*, Nov. 2000.

CHALLENGE:

If you haven't already done so, write down your experience of when you were baptized and how you felt on that special day. Invite your family members who are baptized to do the same and share each other's testimonies.

SEMINARY SCRIPTURE MASTERY:

Psalm 24:3–4   1 Corinthians 15:29
Isaiah 1:18   D&C 137:7–10
John 3:5

PREACH MY GOSPEL:

Pages 2, 9, 40, 63–66, 75, 86, 104–9, 121, 176, 203–8

"Faith and repentance, baptism and bestowal of the Holy Ghost constitute the heart of the gospel of Jesus Christ, being the essential requirements for entry into the celestial kingdom."

—Bruce D. Porter, "The First Principles and Ordinances of the Gospel," *Ensign*, Oct. 2000

"Faith and repentance, baptism and bestowal of the Holy Ghost constitute the heart of the gospel of Jesus Christ, being the essential requirements for entry into the celestial kingdom."

—Bruce D. Porter, "The First Principles and Ordinances of the Gospel," *Ensign*, Oct. 2000

THE GIFT OF THE HOLY GHOST

Music

"The Holy Ghost"—Children's Songbook #105

"The Still Small Voice"—Children's Songbook #106

"Dearest Children, God Is Near You"—*Hymns* #96

"God of Power, God of Right"—*Hymns* #20

"Great is the Lord"—*Hymns* #77

"The Spirit of God"—*Hymns* #2

SUMMARY:

The Holy Ghost has been sent to us by a loving Heavenly Father to provide comfort, guidance, and a witness for truth. The Holy Ghost is a member of the Godhead and has a distinct mission to testify of the Father and the Son to our minds and hearts. The Holy Ghost is a personage of spirit that speaks to our souls, and by its power, we are able to understand and live the gospel of Jesus Christ.

Everyone in the world can feel the influence of the Holy Ghost at certain times; however, the gift of the Holy Ghost is the privilege to receive its constant companionship and guidance by the laying on of hands. The gift of the Holy Ghost is bestowed upon a repentant person whose sins have been washed away at baptism. To hear the quiet promptings of the Holy Ghost we must be obedient, humble, and prayerful. This great gift from a loving Father can bless us with guidance, comfort, and testimony.

QUOTES:

"The simplicity of this ordinance may cause us to overlook its significance. These four words—"Receive the Holy Ghost"—are not a passive pronouncement; rather, they constitute a priesthood injunction—an authoritative admonition to act and not simply to be acted upon" (David A. Bednar, "Receive the Holy Ghost," *Ensign*, Nov. 2010).

"We need the help of the Holy Ghost if we are to make our way safely through what the Apostle Paul called the 'perilous times' in which we now live" (Gerald N. Lund, "Opening Our Hearts," *Ensign*, Apr. 2008).

"When the Prophet Joseph Smith was asked 'wherein [the LDS Church] differed . . . from the other religions of the day,' he replied that it was in 'the gift of the Holy Ghost by the laying on of hands, . . . [and] that all other considerations were contained in the gift of the Holy Ghost' " ("The Light in Their Eyes," James E. Faust, *Ensign*, Nov. 2005).

"The Holy Ghost . . . is our comforter, our direction finder, our communicator, our interpreter, our witness, and our purifier—our infallible guide and sanctifier" (Dallin H. Oaks, "Always Have His Spirit," *Ensign*, Nov. 1996, 59–61).

"Testimony brings to us a knowledge that the gospel is true, but conversion by the Spirit brings something more" (Loren C. Dunn, "Fire and the Holy Ghost," *Ensign*, June 1995, 22–26).

"If [we] would open [our] hearts to the refining influence of this unspeakable gift of the Holy Ghost, a glorious new spiritual dimension would come to light" (Joseph B. Wirthlin, "The Unspeakable Gift," *Ensign*, May 2003, 26–29).

GOSPEL ART:

Boy Samuel Called by the Lord—(111 KIT, 18 GAB)
The Liahona—(302 KIT, 61 GAB)
Abinadi before King Noah—(308 KIT, 75 GAB)

Samuel the Lamanite on the Wall—(314 KIT, 81 GAB)
The Gift of the Holy Ghost—(602 KIT, 105 GAB)
John the Baptist Baptizing Jesus—(208 KIT, 35 GAB)

VIDEOS:

- "The Unspeakable Gift of the Holy Ghost": http://www.lds.org/media-library/video/2012-01-0010-the-unspeakable-gift-of-the-holy-ghost?lang=eng

- "Feeling the Holy Ghost": http://www.lds.org/media-library/video/2012-01-001-feeling-the-holy-ghost?lang=eng

- "Having the Holy Ghost": http://www.lds.org/media-library/video/2012-01-005-having-the-holy-ghost?lang=eng

- There is an excellent 3 part series called "Patterns of Light" by Elder Bednar at: http://www.lds.org/media-library/video/2012-01-011-patterns-of-light-discerning-light?lang=eng

OBJECT LESSONS:

- Have the class listen to the voices of apostles and prophets and try to guess whose voices they are. Then play some voices of members of their family. Talk about how it is much easier to recognize a voice when you are familiar with it. We need to spend time in the scriptures and in prayer in order to recognize the voice of the Lord through the Holy Ghost.

- Show the class a variety of objects that involve air in some way: balloons, a bicycle tire, hair dryer, inflatable balls, air pump, aerosol can, fan, soap bubbles, etc. Ask the class what they have in common. Explain that while we can't see air, we know it's there because of the effects it has on each of those objects. We can't see the Holy Ghost because it doesn't have a physical body, but we can feel its power and influence.

❧ Put a pile of cushions on the floor with a dried pea hidden underneath. Get some volunteers to sit on the cushions and guess what is hidden underneath. You can even tell the class the story about the princess and the pea. The Holy Ghost makes us more sensitive to spiritual things. We are truly sons and daughters of a king.

❧ Demonstrate the difference between the Holy Ghost and the *gift* of the Holy Ghost by using a flashlight. Everyone in the world can feel flashes of inspiration from the Holy Ghost at times when they are receiving comfort, guidance, or a witness of truth; however, it often quickly fades away. Make the flashlight go on and off. After you are baptized and given the gift of the Holy Ghost you have the privilege of having the Holy Ghost as a constant companion. Turn on the flashlight and keep it on. We can keep our spiritual "batteries" charged and receive continuous light from the Holy Ghost if we live worthily.

❧ Show a laptop computer and explain that it has a special device inside that allows it to pick up an Internet signal. If the computer is in range of the signal it has the ability to receive information from all over the world. As baptized members of the Church, we have also been given a special device: the Holy Ghost. When we are in spiritual range, we can receive information from heaven. Talk about some of the things that help us stay in range, as well as those things that keep us from it.

❧ Before class put water in a clear glass and put some hydrogen peroxide in another clear glass. They should look the same to your class. Ask for a volunteer to dip an index finger on each hand into two glasses that contain clear liquid. Now ask the volunteer to rub her fingers with each separate hand until the dipping fingers are dry. One should look the same, while the other one should have some white streaks on it. Ask the class "What is the chemical formula for water?" (H_2O). "What is the chemical formula for hydrogen peroxide?" (H_2O_2). How much difference does one oxygen molecule make? The water represents how we can all feel the Holy Ghost at certain times in our lives. The hydrogen peroxide shows how the *gift* of the Holy Ghost can stay with you.

ARTICLES:

- Douglas L. Callister, "Seeking The Spirit of God," *Ensign*, Nov. 2000.
- Neal A. Maxwell, "The Holy Ghost: Glorifying Christ," *Ensign*, July 2002.
- James E. Faust, "Communion With The Holy Spirit," *Ensign*, Mar. 2002.
- Loren C. Dunn, "Fire and the Holy Ghost," *Ensign*, June 1995.
- Boyd K. Packer, "The Gift of the Holy Ghost: What Every Member Should Know," *Ensign*, Aug. 2006.
- David A. Bednar, "That We May Always Have His Spirit To Be With Us," *Ensign*, May 2006.
- James E. Faust, "The Gift of the Holy Ghost—A Sure Compass," *Ensign*, April 1996.

CHALLENGE:

D&C 8:2 gives us a pattern the Lord uses to help us recognize the Holy Ghost: "Yea, behold, I will tell you in your mind and in your heart, by the Holy Ghost, which shall come upon you and which shall dwell in your heart." Begin a "spiritual journal" where you record your spiritual experiences when you felt the Holy Ghost in your life.

SEMINARY SCRIPTURE MASTERY:

2 Nephi 32:3   D&C 8:2–3

Moroni 10:4–5   D&C 130:22–23

James 1:5–6

PREACH MY GOSPEL:

Pages 18, 90–91

"The Holy Ghost . . . is our comforter, our direction finder, our communicator, our interpreter, our witness, and our purifier—our infallible guide and sanctifier."

—Dallin H. Oaks, "Always Have His Spirit," *Ensign*, Nov. 1996

"The Holy Ghost . . . is our comforter, our direction finder, our communicator, our interpreter, our witness, and our purifier—our infallible guide and sanctifier."

—Dallin H. Oaks, "Always Have His Spirit," *Ensign*, Nov. 1996

ETERNAL MARRIAGE

Music

"Families Can Be Together Forever"—*Hymns #300*
"Children of Our Heavenly Father"—*Hymns #299*
"From Homes of Saints Glad Songs Arise"—*Hymns #297*
"Home Can Be a Heaven on Earth"—*Hymns #298*
"I Am a Child of God"—*Hymns #301*
"Love at Home"—*Hymns #294*

SUMMARY:

Marriage is ordained of God and is between a man and a woman. One of the purposes of marriage is to provide mortal bodies for Heavenly Father's spirit children. Temple marriage is a sacred partnership with God and is essential for exaltation, which is the perfect union of man and woman.

Celestial marriage is the crowning ordinance of the gospel of Jesus Christ. The benefits of a temple marriage are not just eternal, but also bless our mortal life together. Joy in marriage grows sweeter as husband and wife both remain faithful and obedient to gospel covenants. Youth can prepare for eternal marriage as they keep themselves pure and grow spiritually.

Be sensitive to the sisters in the class who may have never married, lost a spouse, or divorced. Remind them the Lord has promised a fulness of blessings to all those who are faithful.

QUOTES:

"One of the most beautiful, comforting doctrines of the Lord— one that brings immense peace, happiness, and unbounded joy—is that principle called eternal marriage. This doctrine means that a man and woman who love each other deeply, who have grown together through the trials, joys, sorrows, and happiness of a shared lifetime, can live beyond the veil together forever with their family who earn that blessing. . . . When there is righteousness, a commitment to give of self, obedience to the commandments of God, and the resolve to seek His will in all things together, that joy is unspeakable" (Richard G. Scott, "Receive the Blessings of the Temple," *Ensign*, May 1999).

"Temple marriage is a covenant that bridges death, transcends time, stretches unbreakable into eternity" (Spencer W. Kimball, "First Presidency Message, Temples and Eternal Marriage," *Ensign*, Aug. 1974, 2–6).

"To those who keep the covenant of marriage, God promises the fulness of His glory, eternal lives, eternal increase, exaltation in the celestial kingdom, and a fulness of joy" (F. Burton Howard, "Eternal Marriage," *Ensign*, May 2003).

"Marriage between a man and a woman is ordained of God, and only through the new and everlasting covenant of marriage can we realize the fulness of all eternal blessings" (David E. Sorensen, "The Honeymoon Trail," *Liahona*, Oct. 1997, 16–19).

"Since life is eternal—and that is absolutely certain—true marriage must also be eternal" (Spencer W. Kimball, "The Role of Righteous Women," *Ensign*, Oct. 1979, 2–6).

"Everything that we do in the Church is connected and associated with and tied into the eternal order of matrimony that God has ordained" (Bruce R. McConkie, "Celestial Marriage," *New Era*, June 1978, 12–17).

GOSPEL ART:

Jesus Christ—(240 KIT, 1 GAB)

Adam and Eve Kneeling at an Altar—(4 GAB)

Adam and Eve Teaching Their Children—5 GAB)

Joseph Resists Potiphar's Wife—(110 KIT, 11 GAB)

The Ten Commandments—(4 GAB)

Ruth Gleaning in the Fields—(17 GAB)

Esther—(21 GAB)

Joseph and Mary Travel to Bethlehem—(29 GAB)

My Father's House—(52 GAB)

Mary and the Resurrected Jesus Christ—(233 KIT, 59 GAB)

Emma Smith—(88 GAB)

Melchizedek Priesthood Restoration—(408 KIT, 94 GAB)

Elijah Appearing in the Kirtland Temple—(95 GAB)

The Foundation of the Relief Society—(98 GAB)

Mary Fielding Smith and Joseph—(412 KIT, 101 GAB)

Kirtland Temple—(500 KIT, 117 GAB)

Nauvoo Illinois Temple—(501 KIT, 118 GAB)

Salt Lake Temple—(502 KIT, 119 GAB)

Young Couple Going to the Temple—(120 GAB)

Temple Baptismal Font—(121 GAB)

VIDEOS:

- "Why Mormons Build Temples": www.lds.org/ldsorg/v/index.jsp?vgnextoid=bd163ca6e9aa3210VgnVCM1000003a94610aRCRD&locale=0

- Video: "Marriage and Divorce": www.lds.org/ldsorg/v/index.jsp?vgnextoid=bd163ca6e9aa3210VgnVCM1000003a94610aRCRD&locale=0

- "Expressions of Love": http://www.lds.org/media-library/video/2011-08-014-expressions-of-love?lang=eng

- "Eternal Marriage": http://www.lds.org/media-library/video /2009-04-014-eternal-marriage-debbie?lang=eng

- "Standing Up: Marriage": http://www.lds.org/media-library /video/2001-08-03-standing-up-marriage?lang=eng

OBJECT LESSONS:

- Have two sisters hold a short string across the front the room, one on each end. Now ask another sister to attach a clothespin to the string, except only give her half of a clothespin. She obviously won't be able to attach it. Give her a complete clothespin and allow her to attach it to the string. Now ask another sister to cut the string with scissors; however, only give her one half of the scissors. Obviously, she won't be able to complete the task. Now give her a real pair of scissors and allow her to cut the string. Both items serve as great analogies for marriage. If only one person is trying to hang on, it won't work; you need both partners to work together. Likewise, if both partners in the marriage choose "cutting" remarks and are always fighting, it won't take long for everything to fall apart.

- Have a husband and wife play pretend Tug-of-War, using a paper chain. The chain represents civil marriage. It doesn't take long to separate if husband and wife are pulling at opposite ends with different goals. If the chain isn't strong, it won't take much for it to break. Now ask the same husband and wife play Tug-of-War, this time using a metal chain, which represents temple marriage. With a strong foundation, even if the couple struggles through life they can hold the marriage together.

- Hold up a donut and compare it to temporal marriage: sweet and delicious, but built around a big hole . . . "til death do us part." Tell the sisters "do-nut settle for a marriage that won't last into the eternities." Pass around cinnamon rolls, comparing those to eternal marriage without a hole.

ARTICLES:

- Spencer W. Kimball, "The Importance of Celestial Marriage," *Ensign*, Oct. 1979, 2–6.
- Bruce C. Hafen, "Covenant Marriage," *Ensign*, Nov. 1996, 26–28.
- F. Burton Howard, "Eternal Marriage," *Ensign*, May 2003, 92–94.
- Spencer W. Kimball, "Temples and Eternal Marriage," *Ensign*, Aug. 1974, 2–6.
- Marion D. Hanks, "Eternal Marriage," *Ensign*, Nov. 1984.
- L. Whitney Clayton, "Marriage: Watch and Learn," *Ensign*, May 2013.

CHALLENGE:

If you are married, write a list of all the good qualities you see in your spouse. Refer to this list when you get frustrated with him! Choose one new act of service you will perform for him this week that you've never done before. Plan your next date night. If you have never been married, pray for patience. Look online for a singles conference you could attend and invite some friends you could attend it with. If you are an older widow, pray for comfort until you and your spouse can be reunited. Discover ways you can use your talents to bless others.

SEMINARY SCRIPTURE MASTERY:

Exodus 20:3–17   D&C 131:1–4

PREACH MY GOSPEL:

Page 86

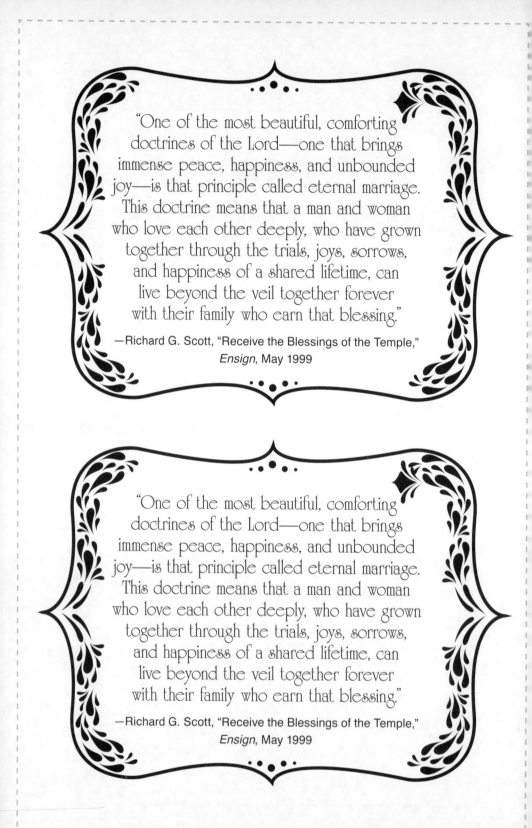

"One of the most beautiful, comforting doctrines of the Lord—one that brings immense peace, happiness, and unbounded joy—is that principle called eternal marriage. This doctrine means that a man and woman who love each other deeply, who have grown together through the trials, joys, sorrows, and happiness of a shared lifetime, can live beyond the veil together forever with their family who earn that blessing."

—Richard G. Scott, "Receive the Blessings of the Temple," *Ensign*, May 1999

"One of the most beautiful, comforting doctrines of the Lord—one that brings immense peace, happiness, and unbounded joy—is that principle called eternal marriage. This doctrine means that a man and woman who love each other deeply, who have grown together through the trials, joys, sorrows, and happiness of a shared lifetime, can live beyond the veil together forever with their family who earn that blessing."

—Richard G. Scott, "Receive the Blessings of the Temple," *Ensign*, May 1999

BRINGING UP CHILDREN IN LIGHT AND TRUTH

Music

"Children All Over the World"—Children's Songbook #16

"Come, Ye Children of the Lord"—*Hymns* #58

"Dearest Children, God Is Near You"—*Hymns* #96

"I Am A Child of God"—*Hymns* #301

"Family Prayer"—Children's Songbook #189

"Teach Me to Walk in the Light"—*Hymns* #304

SUMMARY:

While the Church has some excellent gospel instruction provided by seminary, institute, Sunday School, etc. parents have the ultimate responsibility for raising their children and teaching them truth. Let us not be caught up in the pursuits of worldly activities, that we neglect the spiritual training of our children.

Our faithful examples can help our children to see the joy in righteous living so that they desire the same life and blessings. We can bear our testimonies much better with our actions than our words. We should use not only the designated Family Home Evening time to teach gospel principles, but also any time during the day or night when our children's hearts are open. Parents need to introduce gospel truths starting when their children are very young, teaching them prayer, a love for the scriptures, a commitment to virtue and integrity, and a desire to serve missions and receive temple ordinances.

Recent leaders of the Church have warned us that our current home instruction will not be enough to fortify our homes against the adversary in the last days; it is time to clothe them in the armor of God hourly and bathe them in light and truth. If we do, our families will be protected and filled with peace, despite the turbulent world that surrounds us.

QUOTES:

"Of all the joys of life, none other equals that of happy parenthood. Of all the responsibilities with which we struggle, none other is so serious. To rear children in an atmosphere of love, security, and faith is the most rewarding of all challenges. The good result from such efforts becomes life's most satisfying compensation" (Gordon B. Hinckley, "Save the Children," *Ensign*, Nov. 1994, 54).

"Never forget that these little ones are the sons and daughters of God and that yours is a custodial relationship to them, that He was a parent before you were parents and that He has not relinquished His parental rights or interest in these little ones. Now, love them, take care of them. Fathers, control your tempers, now and in all the years to come. Mothers, control your voices, keep them down. Rear your children in love, in the nurture and admonition of the Lord. Take care of your little ones, welcome them into your homes and nurture and love them with all of your hearts" (Gordon B. Hinckley, Salt Lake University Third Stake Conference, 3 Nov. 1996; in *Church News*, 1 Mar. 1997, 2).

"When our Heavenly Father sends one of his spirit children into a home, it is as if he says to the parents: "John, Mary, here is my most priceless possession—the soul of a little child. As you can see, he is helpless and completely dependent upon you even for life itself. You are now given the privilege of molding his life as you think best. Please teach him that I am his Father and that Jesus is his Savior and that we want him and you to return and live with us when mortality is over. Remember that I am always available to guide you in rearing this child of ours if you will but seek my help. I hope you will do so often. Your Heavenly Father" (H. Verlan Andersen, "Bring Up Your Children in Light and Truth," *Ensign*, Nov. 1991).

"The Lord has given us the charge to 'bring up [our] children in light and truth.' May we respond to this charge with faith and determination to fulfill our duty to the rising generation" (Robert D. Hales, "Our Parental Duty to God and to the Rising Generation," *Ensign*, Aug. 2010).

"It is not enough simply to provide food and shelter for the physical being. There is an equal responsibility to provide nourishment and direction to the spirit and the mind and the heart. Wrote Paul to Timothy, 'But if any provide not for his own, and specially for those of his own house, he hath denied the faith, and is worse than an infidel' (1 Tim 5:8)" (Gordon B. Hinckley, "Bring Up a Child in the Way He Should Go," *Ensign*, Nov. 1993).

GOSPEL ART:

Boy Samuel Called by the Lord—(111 KIT, 18 GAB)
Adam and Eve Teaching Their Children—(119 KIT, 4 GAB)
Jacob Blessing His Sons—(122 KIT, 12 GAB)
Boy Jesus in the Temple—(205 KIT, 34 GAB)
Childhood of Jesus Christ—(206 KIT)
Jesus Praying With His Mother—(33 GAB)
Captain Moroni Raises the Title of Liberty—(312 KIT, 79 GAB)
Two Thousand Young Warriors—(313 KIT, 80 GAB)
Jesus Blesses the Nephite Children—(322 KIT, 84 GAB)
Joseph Smith Seeks Wisdom in the Bible—(402 KIT, 89 GAB)
Helping the Martin Handcart Company across the Sweetwater River—
    (415 KIT)
Temple Baptismal Font—(504 KIT, 121 GAB)
Passing the Sacrament—(604 KIT, 108 GAB)
Young Boy Praying—(605 KIT, 111 GAB)
Family Prayer—(606 KIT, 112 GAB)
Young Girl Speaking at Church—(607 KIT)
Christ and Children from around the World—(608 KIT, 116 GAB)
Family Togetherness—(616 KIT)
Search the Scriptures—(617 KIT)

VIDEOS:

- ❧ "Courageous Parenting": http://www.lds.org/media-library /video/2010-10-5030-elder-larry-r-lawrence?lang=eng

- ❧ "Parenting: Touching the Hearts of Our Youth": http://www.lds. org/media-library/video/2010-08-15-parenting-touching-the-hearts-of-our-youth?lang=eng

- ❧ "Children": http://www.lds.org/media-library/video/2011-10 -2030-elder-neil-l-andersen?lang=eng

- ❧ "Becoming Children of Christ": http://lds.org/library/display /0,4945,6635-1-4786-2,00.html

- ❧ "Building Up a Righteous Posterity": http://lds.org/library/ display/0,4945,6635-1-4786-9,00.html

- ❧ "Proclamation": http://lds.org/media-library/video/prophets -and-apostles-speak-today?lang=eng

OBJECT LESSONS:

- ❧ Ask for a volunteer to mold something out of clay. Once she has shown her masterpiece to the class, ask her to mold something out of a flower. Obviously, she won't be able to do that. Tell her to try harder. Explain that we have the power and opportunity to mold our own life, but that we can't force our children or spouse to be what they are not. It is fruitless and even damaging to try to mold the flower into something different. Force is not the Lord's plan. Providing the best circumstances for blooming is the Lord's plan.

- ❧ Ask for a volunteer to come up to the room to get the absolute best cake in the world. Uncover a plate with a teeny, tiny piece on it. Explain that this cake has the finest ingredients in the world. Ask the class how they feel about quantity versus quality. Are both required in good parenting? How big should our serving of gospel instruction in our homes be for our children?

❧ Set two buckets on the table in the front of the room, one filled with water and one empty. Ask the class to call out things that make us frustrated or discouraged during a typical day. For each thing they name, take a cup of water out of the full bucket. Explain that we are like that bucket; when things happen during the day that defeat us, a cup of self-esteem and inner peace is taken out. Now, ask the class for suggestions on how we can help a person whose bucket is empty. With each suggestion, pour a cup of water into the empty bucket. Talk about how our homes should be where our buckets are consistently filled each day.

ARTICLES:

❧ H. Verlan Andersen, "Bring Up Your Children in Light and Truth," *Ensign*, Nov. 1991.

❧ Robert D. Hales, "Our Parental Duty to God and to the Rising Generation," *Liahona*, Aug. 2010.

❧ Marion G. Romney, "Let Us Set in Order Our Own Houses," *Ensign*, Jan. 1985.

❧ James E. Faust, "The Greatest Challenge in the World—Good Parenting," *Ensign*, Nov. 1990.

❧ Gordon B. Hinckley, "Bring Up A Child in the Way He Should Go," *Ensign*, Nov. 1993.

CHALLENGE:

If you have children, write them each a letter, highlighting all of their good qualities and emphasizing how much you love them. Bear your testimony of the Savior in the letter. If your parents are still alive, do the same for them. If you do not have any children, write the name of a family you can serve this week and what you will do.

SEMINARY SCRIPTURE MASTERY:

2 Nephi 2:27	1 Corinthians 10:13
2 Nephi 28–29	Revelation 20:12–13
2 Nephi 28:7–9	D&C 14:7
Mosiah 3:19	D&C 58:26–27
Mosiah 4:30	D&C 59:9–10
Alma 34:32–34	D&C 82:3
Alma 37:35	D&C 82:10
Alma 41:10	D&C 88:123–24
3 Nephi 27:27	D&C 89:18–21
Moroni 7:16–17	D&C 130:18–19
Matthew 5:14–16	D&C 130:20–21

PREACH MY GOSPEL:

Pages 3, 21, 32, 85, 159–60, 164

"Of all the joys of life, none other equals that of happy parenthood. Of all the responsibilities with which we struggle, none other is so serious. To rear children in an atmosphere of love, security, and faith is the most rewarding of all challenges."

—Gordon B. Hinckley,
"Save the Children,"
Ensign, Nov. 1994

"Of all the joys of life, none other equals that of happy parenthood. Of all the responsibilities with which we struggle, none other is so serious. To rear children in an atmosphere of love, security, and faith is the most rewarding of all challenges."

—Gordon B. Hinckley,
"Save the Children,"
Ensign, Nov. 1994

SEALING POWER AND TEMPLE BLESSINGS

Music

"God Is in His Holy Temple"—*Hymns* #132
"High on the Mountain Top"—*Hymns* #5
"Holy Temples on Mount Zion"—*Hymns* #289
"How Beautiful Thy Temples, Lord"—*Hymns* #288
"We Love Thy House, O God"—"*Hymns* #247

SUMMARY:

Sacred temples are built as a school for the Saints to receive eternal ordinances, make important covenants, and gain vital knowledge that will bind their families together forever and allow them to enter the celestial kingdom. Elijah restored the sealing power to the earth so that it would not be utterly wasted at the Lord's Second Coming.

Salvation is given to every living man and woman, but exaltation requires that everyone be baptized and receive temple ordinances. For those who have lived on earth without hearing the gospel and receiving the saving ordinances, others can perform the temple work on their behalf. Our ancestors gave us the gift of life, and by doing their temple work we can help them gain eternal life. A merciful Father in Heaven allows us to receive those endowments for our kindred dead and make eternal blessings available to our ancestors who were not able to enter the temple for themselves.

As we research our family's history to identify our ancestors, the Lord will help us. He wants families to be together and has given us the tools we need, including the sacred houses where they can be sealed. It is one of the most important works we can do here on earth. Our deceased loved ones are counting on us to help them with their eternal progression. If you want to have a spiritual experience, do your genealogy.

QUOTES:

"It is a place of peace, solitude, and inspiration. Regular attendance will enrich your life with greater purpose. It will permit you to provide deceased ancestors the exalting ordinances you have received. Go to the temple. You know it is the right thing to do. Do it now" (Richard G. Scott, "Receive the Blessings of the Temple," *Ensign*, May 1999).

"Genealogies, family stories, historical accounts, and traditions . . . form a bridge between past and future and bind generations together in ways that no other keepsake can" (Dennis B. Neuenschwander, "Holy Place, Sacred Space," *Liahona*, July 1999, 98–100).

"If you don't know [your family's] history, then you don't know anything. You are a leaf that doesn't know it is part of a tree" (Michael Chrichton).

"There exists a righteous unity between the temple and the home. Understanding the eternal nature of the temple will draw you to your family; understanding the eternal nature of the family will draw you to the temple" (Gary E. Stevenson, "Sacred Homes, Sacred Temples," Ensign, May 2009, 102).

"In the ordinances of the temple, the foundations of the eternal family are sealed in place" (Howard W. Hunter, "A Temple-Motivated People," *Liahona*, May 1995, 4).

"The Lord has trusted you by letting you hear the gospel in your lifetime, giving you the chance to accept the obligation to offer it to those of your ancestors who did not have your priceless opportunity. Think of the gratitude He has for those who pay the price in work and faith to find the names of their ancestors and who love them and Him enough to offer them eternal life in families, the greatest of all the gifts of God. He offered them an infinite sacrifice. He will love and appreciate those who paid whatever price they could to allow their ancestors to choose

His offer of eternal life" (Henry B. Eyring, "Hearts Bound Together," *Ensign*, May 2005, 79).

GOSPEL ART:

Jesus Christ—(240 KIT, 1 GAB)
Boy Jesus in the Temple—(205 KIT, 34 GAB)
Jesus Cleansing the Temple—(224 KIT, 51 GAB)
My Father's House—(GAP 52)
Melchizedek Priesthood Restoration—(GAB 94)
Elijah Appearing in the Kirtland Temple—(GAB 95)
Kirtland Temple—(500 KIT, 117 GAB)
Nauvoo Illinois Temple—(501 KIT, 118 GAB)
Salt Lake Temple—(502 KIT, 119 GAB)
Young Couple Going to the Temple—(609 KIT, 120 GAP)
Temple Baptismal Font—(504 KIT, 121 GAB)
Temple Used Anciently—(118 KIT)
Elijah Restores the Power to Seal Families for Eternity—(417 KIT)
Nauvoo Temple—(118 GAB)
Washington DC Temple—(505 KIT)

VIDEOS:

- "Temple Mirrors of Eternity": http://www.lds.org/media-library/video/general-conference-october-2010?lang=eng&start=25&end=36#2010-10-2060-elder-gerrit-w-gong

- "Why Mormons Build Temples": www.lds.org/ldsorg/v/index.jsp?vgnextoid=bd163ca6e9aa3210VgnVCM1000003a94610aRCRD&locale=0

- "Endowed with Power": http://lds.org/library/display/0,4945,6635-1-4786-3,00.html

- "The Blessings of the Temple": http://lds.org/media-library /video/mormon-messages?lang=eng#2009-02-04-the-message-of -the-restoration

- "Why Mormons Build Temples": http://lds.org/media-library /video/our-faith?lang=eng&start=13&end=24

- "Why Mormons Do Family History": http://lds.org/media -library/video/our-values?lang=eng

- "Eternal Family" (several on this page): http://lds.org/media -library/video/truth-restored?lang=eng&start=25&end=36

OBJECT LESSONS:

- Have a talent contest to see who can comb their hair without bending their elbows or talk on a cell phone without touching it? Ask two sisters to eat a candy bar without bending their elbows. What's the punch line? It can't be done, unless they help each other. Our ancestors need us as much as we needed them. Together, we save each other.

- Invite your ward Family History Specialist to share some special experiences about binding heaven with earth.

- Show the class several items (or pictures of items): candy, coins, $20 bill, stuffed animal, diamond ring. Ask the class which item they think a baby would be most interested in. (Candy and toy.) Ask why the baby wouldn't select the most expensive item? (She doesn't understand the value of it.) Talk about how some people don't understand the value of temples, so they make choices that might prevent them from being worthy to enter the temple.

- Invite your ward's Family History Specialist to show your class how to use the Church's new Family Tree online. Search for an ancestor of someone in the class. Another option is to invite the ward's Family History Index Specialist to show how the sisters can do indexing work online or even on their cell phones with the fun mobile app.

ARTICLES:

- Dallin H. Oaks, "Family History: 'In Wisdom and Order,' " *Ensign*, June 1989, 6–8.
- Boyd K. Packer, "Your Family History: Getting Started," *Ensign*, Aug. 2003, 12–17.
- Russell M. Nelson, "Prepare for Blessings of the Temple," *Ensign*, Mar. 2002, 17.
- David E. Sorensen, "The Doctrine of Temple Work," *Liahona*, Aug. 2002, 30.
- Howard W. Hunter, "A Temple-Motivated People," *Ensign*, May 1995.
- Stacy Vickery, "Temple Blessings Now and Eternally," *Liahona*, Sept. 2011.
- Richard G. Scott, "Receive the Temple Blessings," *Ensign*, May 1999.
- Howard W. Hunter, "We Have A Work To Do," *Ensign*, Mar. 1995, 64–65.
- Dennis B. Neuenschwander, "Bridges and Eternal Keepsakes," *Ensign*, May 1999, 83–85.

CHALLENGE:

Watch the tutorial videos on the Church's new "Family Tree" website at www.FamilySearch.org. Click on "Family Tree" in the top menu. If you don't have one already, create an account and begin researching the names of your ancestors to see where you can begin doing their temple work.

SEMINARY SCRIPTURE MASTERY:

Job 19:25–26   D&C 131:1–4
1 Corinthians 15:20–22   D&C 131:1–4
1 Corinthians 15:29   D&C 137:7–10

PREACH MY GOSPEL:

Page 86

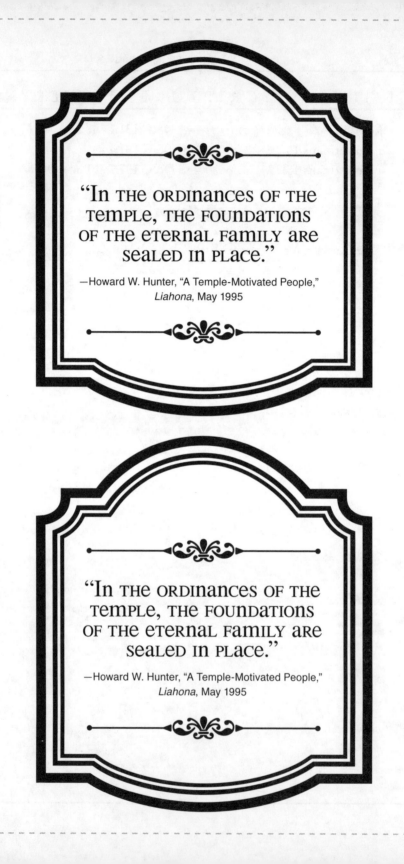

"In the ordinances of the temple, the foundations of the eternal family are sealed in place."

—Howard W. Hunter, "A Temple-Motivated People," *Liahona*, May 1995

"In the ordinances of the temple, the foundations of the eternal family are sealed in place."

—Howard W. Hunter, "A Temple-Motivated People," *Liahona*, May 1995

LESSON EIGHTEEN

LIVING BY EVERY WORD THAT PROCEEDS FROM THE MOUTH OF GOD

Music

"Choose the Right"—*Hymns #239*

"Come, Follow Me"—*Hymns #116*

"Do What is Right"—*Hymns #237*

"How Gentle God's Commands"—*Hymns #125*

"I'll Go Where You Want Me to Go"—*Hymns #270*

"Keep the Commandments"—*Hymns #303*

SUMMARY:

Because God is our loving Father in Heaven, He knows what is best for our eternal progression, and so He gives us commandments to protect us along our earthly journey. He knows what will ultimately make us happy. In exchange for His guidance, we give Him our obedience. God governs the universe by law and order, and we are subject to that law. Commandments are designed to steer us away from things that will harm or destroy us spiritually or physically. Obedience blesses us with additional strength and increased faith.

Obedience is a measure of our commitment to God. Obeying out of love is better than obeying out of fear; our attitude reveals our level of spirituality.

When we obey a particular law, we are entitled to the blessings that are promised. Hypocrisy is when we go to church one day and act like non-believers the other six days of the week. We can't live worldly lives and then expect heavenly rewards.

QUOTES:

"All who seek full happiness can find it in the gospel of Jesus Christ, taught in His Church. . . . As we keep His commandments, we are blessed and come to know true happiness. We learn that happiness lies in doing small things that build us up, that increase our faith and testimony" (Claudio R. M. Costa, "Fun and Happiness," *Ensign*, Nov. 2002).

"As a person studies the words of the Lord and obeys them, he or she draws closer to the Savior and obtains a greater desire to live a righteous life" (Merrill J. Bateman, "Coming unto Christ by Searching the Scriptures," *Ensign*, Nov. 1992, 27–28).

"Reading and studying the scriptures make us conscious of the many conditional promises made by the Lord to encourage obedience and righteous living" (Howard W. Hunter, *Ensign*, Nov. 1982, 57–58).

"One goal that most of us share in this life is the desire to achieve true joy and lasting happiness. There is only one way to do this, and that is by being obedient to all the commandments of God" (Delbert L. Stapley, "The Blessings of Righteous Obedience," *Ensign*, Nov. 1977, 18–21).

"Obedience leads to true freedom. The more we obey revealed truth, the more we become liberated" (James E. Faust, "Obedience: The Path to Freedom," *Ensign*, May 1999, 45–47).

"To achieve your goals in this mortal life and prove yourselves worthy of eternal blessings, learn to obey. There is no other way" (Joseph B. Wirthlin, "Live in Obedience," *Ensign*, May 1994, 39–42).

GOSPEL ART:

Adam and Eve Kneeling at an Altar—(4 GAB)

Adam and Eve Teaching Their Children—(5 GAB)

City of Zion is Taken Up—(6 GAB)

Building the Ark—(102 KIT, 7 GAB)

Noah and the Ark with Animals—103 KIT, 8 GAB)

Abraham Taking Isaac to be Sacrificed—(105 KIT, 9 GAB)

Joseph Resists Potiphar's Wife—(110 KIT, 11 GAB)

Moses and the Burning Bush—(107 KIT, 13 GAB)

The Ten Commandments—(14 GAB)

Moses and the Brass Serpent—(16 GAB)

Boy Samuel Called by the Lord—(111 KIT, 18 GAB)

Esther—(21 GAB)

Daniel Refusing the King's Food and Wine—(114 KIT, 23 GAB)

Three Men in the Fiery Furnace—(116 KIT, 25 GAB)

Daniel in the Lions' Den—(117 KIT, 26 GAB)

Jonah—(27 GAB)

John the Baptist Baptizing Jesus—(208 KIT, 35 GAB)

Calling of the Fishermen—(209 KIT, 37 GAB)

Jesus Calms the Storm—(214 KIT, 40 GAB)

Jesus Raising Jairus's Daughter—(215 KIT, 41 GAB)

Mary and Martha—(45 GAB)

Christ and the Rich Young Ruler—(48 GAB)

Jesus Raising Lazarus from the Dead—(222 KIT, 49 GAB)

Two Thousand Young Warriors—(313 KIT, 80 GAB)

Brother Joseph—(400 KIT, 87 GAB)

Blessing the Sacrament—(107 GAB)

Missionaries: Elders—(109 GAB)

Missionaries: Sisters—(110 GAB)

Family Prayer—(112 GAB)

Payment of Tithing—(113 GAB)

Young Couple Going to the Temple—(120 GAB)

VIDEOS:

- "Windows of Heaven Open to Obedient": http://www.lds.org/ media-library/video/2010-07-093-windows-of-heaven-open-to-obedient?lang=eng

- "The Lord's Way": http://www.lds.org/media-library/video /2013-04-2060-elder-stanley-g-ellis?lang=eng

- "Arabian Horse": http://www.lds.org/media-library/video/2011-03-100-arabian-horse?lang=eng

- "Safety Lies in Obeying the Prophets": http://www.lds.org/ media-library/video/2012-08-1910-safety-lies-in-obeying-the-prophets?lang=eng

OBJECT LESSONS:

- Ask someone to read the recipe for chocolate chip cookies while you make them for the class. When "oil" is mentioned, add some car oil. When "flour" is read aloud, toss some flowers into the bowl. Add potato chips instead of chocolate chips. Instead of baking soda, toss in some soda pop. Use garlic salt when "salt" is mentioned. Of course, by now your class will be groaning. Talk about how when the Lord asks us to be obedient, we can't pick and choose how we'll interpret the commandments.

- Decorate the room with kites and explain how the parts of a kite can teach us about obedience. The structure of the kite represents the gospel. The tail symbolizes balance in our lives and the wind represents trials we pass through. The string, which symbolizes commandments, is what holds the kite up in the sky. Commandments are not meant to tie us down; soaring can only be done when you hold onto the string. The string of the gospel keeps us safe and in control. If we ever cut that string, and decide obeying God's laws is too much trouble, then eventually we will lose control and do a nose dive.

- Wrap an egg in bubble-wrap and tissue and then drop it on the floor. The soft packaging should protect the egg, which would have broken by itself. The gospel is designed to protect each of us in the same way—by helping us build layers of testimony as we keep the commandments.

- Create a Family Home Evening packet about keeping the commandments. Invite the class to cut out pictures, color visual aids, and prepare the material to use at home with their families while you teach the lesson.

- Invite a Seminary teacher to show the class different methods of marking scriptures and building scripture chains. You could even teach them how to do a Scripture Chase competition like they do in Seminary.

ARTICLES:

- Joseph B. Wirthlin, "Live in Obedience," *Ensign*, May 1994, 39–42.
- Gordon B. Hinckley, "If Ye Be Willing and Obedient," *Ensign*, July 1995, 2–5.
- Thomas S. Monson, "Strength through Obedience," *Ensign*, July 1996, 2–5.
- Donald L. Staheli, "Obedience—Life's Great Challenge," *Ensign*, May 1998, 81–82.
- Delbert L. Stapley, "The Blessings of Righteous Obedience," *Ensign*, Nov. 1977, 18–21.

CHALLENGE:

Think about all of the commandments and evaluate how you are doing. Choose one that you could do better at and commit to living it perfectly. Teach a Family Home Evening lesson about that particular commandment and its promised blessings to your family this week.

SEMINARY SCRIPTURE MASTERY:

1 Nephi 19:23

2 Nephi 9:28–29

2 Nephi 32:3

Mosiah 3:19

Alma 37:35

Helaman 5:12

Moroni 7:16–17

Exodus 20:3–17

Joshua 1:8

Joshua 24:15

Ezekiel 37:15–17

Matthew 5:14–16

John 7:17

John 14:15

2 Timothy 3:16–17

D&C 14:7

PREACH MY GOSPEL:

Pages 7, 24, 38–39, 73–74, 103–108, 130, 180–82

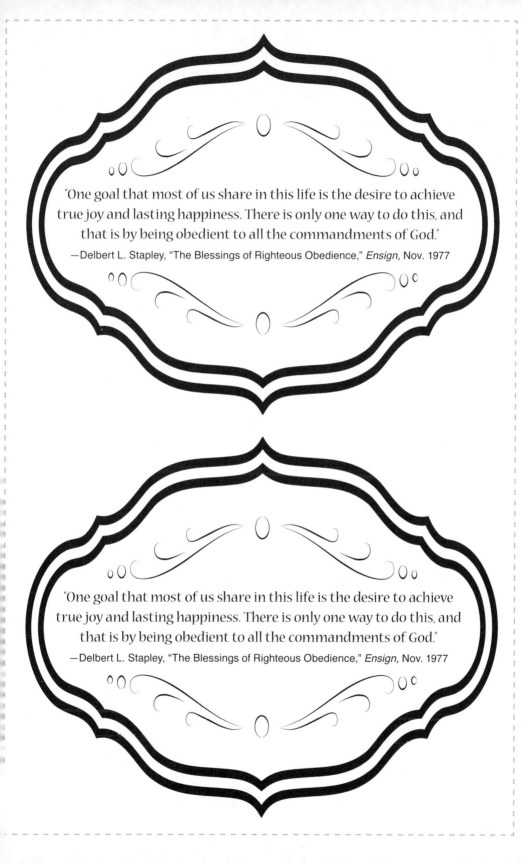

"One goal that most of us share in this life is the desire to achieve true joy and lasting happiness. There is only one way to do this, and that is by being obedient to all the commandments of God."
—Delbert L. Stapley, "The Blessings of Righteous Obedience," *Ensign,* Nov. 1977

"One goal that most of us share in this life is the desire to achieve true joy and lasting happiness. There is only one way to do this, and that is by being obedient to all the commandments of God."
—Delbert L. Stapley, "The Blessings of Righteous Obedience," *Ensign,* Nov. 1977

IN THE WORLD BUT NOT OF THE WORLD

Music
"Behold! A Royal Army"—*Hymns #251*
"I'll Go Where You Want Me"—*Hymns #270*
"Let Us All Press On"—*Hymns #243*
"True to the Faith"—*Hymns #254*
"We Are All Enlisted"—*Hymns #250*
"Who's On the Lord's Side"—*Hymns #260*

SUMMARY:

The Lord isn't waiting for the world to become darker before He comes again; He is waiting for His saints to shine brighter. Wickedness is increasing at an ever rapid pace, and our homes and values are being assaulted on every side. Still, the positive influence members of the Church can have around them can be very powerful if we are not afraid to stand as a witness of Christ and step away from worldliness. We can prevent the adversary from having any power over our homes and hearts by obeying the Lord's loving commandments.

We will be safe and happy when we stay within the Lord's boundaries. Our challenge during mortality is to choose the joyful eternal kingdom of God rather than temporary earthly pleasures. God promises specific blessings when we obey certain commandments. For example, we receive divine protection from consequences when we keep the Sabbath day holy, obey the Word of Wisdom, respect the name of Deity, and keep the Law of Chastity.

What good is having someone who can walk on water if you don't follow in His footsteps? With the Lord's help, we can improve ourselves each day. Through repentance and the Atonement of Jesus Christ, we can start over and try again.

Relief Society sisters need to be courageous to step into their communities to be an influence for good. We shouldn't be surprised or afraid as the world becomes more terrifying; it has been prophesied to be so, but it has also been shown to prophets of old that we would stand strong and protect that which is good and righteous. The gospel of Jesus Christ is the only thing that will bring peace to the world; the Prince of Peace is the answer to the earth's woes.

QUOTES:

"Gospel doctrine makes it clear that we must live in this world to achieve our eternal destination. We must be tried and tested and found worthy of a greater kingdom" (Quentin L. Cook, "Being in the World but Not of the World," *Youth*, online).

"For members of this Church to enjoy the blessings of a covenant people, the law of the Lord must be written in their hearts" (James E. Faust, "Search Me, O God, and Know My Heart," *Ensign*, May 1998).

"Our honest effort to keep our covenants allows God to increase our power to do it" (Henry B. Eyring, "Witnesses for God," *Ensign*, Nov. 1996, 30–33).

"Some of us are too content with what we may already be doing. We stand back in the "eat, drink, and be merry" mode when opportunities for growth and development abound" (James E. Faust, "I Believe I Can, I Knew I Could," *Liahona*, Nov. 2002).

"We need not be dismayed if our earnest efforts toward perfection now seem so arduous and endless. Perfection is pending. It can come in full only after the Resurrection and only through the Lord. It awaits all who love him and keep his commandments" (Russell M. Nelson, "Perfection Pending," *Ensign*, Oct. 1995).

"These are the last days. As foretold by God's holy prophets since the world began, they are challenging times, and they are going to become even more challenging. Satan's sole purpose is to make you and me as miserable as he is, and the best way for him to accomplish that is to entice us into disobedience. Although there are all kinds of misery in this world, the only kind that is eternal is misery of the soul. And that kind of misery is centered in sin and transgression" (M. Russell Ballard, "When Shall These Things Be?" *Ensign*, Dec. 1996).

GOSPEL ART:

Three Men in the Fiery Furnace—(116 KIT, 25 GAB)
Daniel in the Lions' Den—(117 KIT, 26 GAB)
Two Thousand Young Warriors—(313 KIT, 80 GAB)
Samuel the Lamanite on the Wall—(314 KIT, 81 GAB)
Joseph Smith in Liberty Jail—(97 GAB)
Noah and the Ark with Animals—(103 KIT, 8 GAB)
Joseph Resists Potiphar's Wife—(110 KIT)
David Slays Goliath—(112 KIT, 19 GAB)
Daniel Refusing the King's Meat and Wine—(114 KIT, 23 GAB)
Enoch and His People Are Taken Up to God—(120 KIT)
Calling of the Fishermen—(209 KIT, 37 GAB)
Jesus at the Door—(237 KIT, 65 GAB)
Christ and the Rich Young Ruler—(244 KIT, 48 GAB)
The Anti-Nephi-Lehies Burying Their Swords—(311 KIT)
Moses and the Brass Serpent—(123 KIT, 16 GAB)
Calling of the Fishermen—(209 KIT, 37 GAB)
Christ Ordaining the Apostles—(211 KIT, 38 GAB)
Lehi's Family Leaving Jerusalem—(301 KIT)
King Benjamin Addresses His People—(307 KIT, 74 GAB)
Alma Baptizes in the Waters of Mormon—(309 KIT, 76 GAB)

VIDEOS:

- ❧ "Follow the Doctrine and Gospel of Christ," M. Russell Ballard: http://www.lds.org/media-library/video/ces-firesides?lang=eng #2010-11-0050-follow-the-doctrine-and-gospel-of-christ

- ❧ "The Dedication of a Lifetime," Dallin H. Oaks: http://www. lds.org/media-library/video/ces-firesides?lang=eng&start=25&e nd=36#2005-05-03-the-dedication-of-a-lifetime

- ❧ "Come Out of the Darkness into the Light," James E. Faust: http://www.lds.org/media-library/video/ces-firesides?lang=eng &start=37&end=48#2002-09-05-come-out-of-the-darkness-into -the-light

- ❧ "Reflections on a Consecrated Life": http://www.lds.org/media-library/video/general-conference-october-2010?lang=eng&start =13&end=24#2010-10-1060-elder-d-todd-christofferson

- ❧ "Choose This Day": http://mormonchannel.org/video?v=911129 092001

OBJECT LESSONS:

- ❧ Display small bowls that contain various white powdery substances, such as baking soda, baking powder, pancake mix, flour, sugar, salt. In another bowl put some powdered lime for the garden or powdered chalk. Tell the class that all of them but one came from the kitchen and are edible. Ask the class which ones are safe to eat. They probably won't be able to tell. Some people say they are Christians, but unless they're truly following the Savior and making covenants with Him, the Lord will "spew them out of His mouth."

- ❧ Bring a weasel ball (can be found at toy stores) and another ball. When turned on, the weasel ball goes all over the place by itself. What kind of member are you? Lively or lifeless? The Lord's covenant people show who they are by their actions and willingness to do His will.

❧ Invite the class to move their right food in a clockwise circle. While they continue to move their foot, ask them to move their left index finger in a counter-clockwise direction. Tell the class that this experiment illustrates that we can't say we're following God, yet do the opposite. Our souls will know it's a lie and will feel uncomfortable.

❧ Show a variety of tools: scale, ruler, measuring cups, spoons, thermometer, voltage detector, stop watch, carpenter's level, etc. Ask the class what all of the things have in common. They are all used to measure things. Ask how we measure true discipleship. The Lord's true followers make covenants with Him to show their dedication and love. John 14:15 says, "If ye love me, keep my commandments."

❧ Invite the class to sing "I am a Child of God" and then tell them the story behind the words. Originally the words read "Teach me all that I must *know* to live with Him someday," but President Spencer W. Kimball said that that's not enough–we have to DO.

❧ Hand someone in the class a pencil and ask her to "try to drop it." When the person drops it, say, "No, I said to TRY to drop it. Have them keep "trying" until they finally catch on that they're really not supposed to drop it. Explain to the class that there is no "TRY"—either you do it or you don't. You either obey and keep the commandments or you don't.

❧ Demonstrate various electric tools and appliances without plugging them in:
  + Use your electric screw driver to turn a screw with your fingers.
  + Mix a drink with a spoon, using your blender.

‣ Sit in front of a fan that is off, fanning yourself with your hand

‣ Sharpen your pencil by hand next to an electric pencil sharpener.

Explain how useful these tools are. Of course someone will probably speak up and tell you that you're not using them correctly and without the power on. Compare that to when we have been given a commandment, but don't ask the Lord for His power or help to live it.

❧ Set up a game of "Jenga," "Stak Attack" or simply stack up wooden blocks in a weave pattern where you pull out the blocks and re-stack them on top until the tower tumbles. Invite class members to remove one of the blocks and mention a commandment we need to obey. As you play the game, discuss the consequences of disobedience. Eventually, the tower will fall and so will our spirituality when we continue to choose evil over good.

ARTICLES:

❧ L. Tom Perry, "In the World," *Ensign*, May 1988.

❧ April Moody, "In Tune With His Will," *Ensign*, Feb. 2006.

❧ L. Tom Perry, "The Tradition of a Balanced, Righteous Life," *Liahona*, Aug. 2011.

❧ Boyd K. Packer, "The Test," *Ensign*, Nov. 2008.

❧ Teddy E. Brewerton, "Obedience—Full Obedience," *Ensign*, May 1981.

❧ Thomas S. Monson, "Obedience Brings Blessings," *Ensign*, May 2013.

CHALLENGE:

Think of one way you are still holding on to the world in your life. Decide how you will step away from it and move toward strict obedience.

Decide what blessing you would like in your life and then find which gospel law promises that particular blessing upon obedience to its principles.

SEMINARY SCRIPTURE MASTERY:

2 Nephi 2:27	Matthew 6:24
2 Nephi 28:7–9	Matthew 25:40
Mosiah 3:19	1 Corinthians 10:13
Mosiah 4:30	2 Timothy 3:1–5
Alma 34:32–34	Revelation 20:12–13
Alma 41:10	D&C 14:7
Helaman 5:12	D&C 58:26–27
3 Nephi 27:27	D&C 59:9–10
Ether 12:27	D&C 82:3
Moses 7:18	D&C 82:10
Psalm 24:3–4	D&C 88:123–24
Matthew 5:14–16	D&C 130:20–21

PREACH MY GOSPEL:

Pages 66, 70, 88

"Gospel doctrine makes it clear that we must live in this world to achieve our eternal destination. We must be tried and tested and found worthy of a greater kingdom."

—Quentin L. Cook, "Being in the World but Not of the World," *Youth*, online

"Gospel doctrine makes it clear that we must live in this world to achieve our eternal destination. We must be tried and tested and found worthy of a greater kingdom."

—Quentin L. Cook, "Being in the World but Not of the World," *Youth*, online

"Gospel doctrine makes it clear that we must live in this world to achieve our eternal destination. We must be tried and tested and found worthy of a greater kingdom."

—Quentin L. Cook, "Being in the World but Not of the World," *Youth*, online

"Gospel doctrine makes it clear that we must live in this world to achieve our eternal destination. We must be tried and tested and found worthy of a greater kingdom."

—Quentin L. Cook, "Being in the World but Not of the World," *Youth*, online

LOVE AND CONCERN FOR ALL OUR FATHER'S CHILDREN

Music

"A Poor Wayfaring Man of Grief"—*Hymns #29*
"As Sisters in Zion" (Women)—*Hymns #309*
"Because I Have Been Given Much"—*Hymns #219*
"I Have Work Enough to Do"—*Hymns #224*
"Sweet Is the Work"—*Hymns #147*
"Love One Another"—*Hymns #308*

SUMMARY:

How can you tell if someone is a true disciple of Jesus Christ? By the way she treats other people. One way we show the Lord how much we love Him is by serving His children, our brothers and sisters. When we feel God's love deep inside our soul, we feel a desire to reach outside ourselves and bless others. A true understanding of the gospel of Jesus Christ compels us to love and serve.

If we want to be like Christ, we need to do as Christ did: serve others. The Savior ministered daily to the needs of those around Him. When we open our spiritual eyes, we will see many opportunities around us for Christ-like service and love. The act of serving others helps the Lord accomplish His work and makes us more like Him. The Lord uses us to bless those around us.

Charity is the pure love of Christ and the greatest of all virtues. Charity cannot be developed in the abstract; it requires clinical, hands-on experience. It is a process, not an event. The more we serve others the more genuine our love will become for others.

QUOTES:

"I am convinced that true brotherly love is essential to our happiness and to world peace. We need to show our love, beginning in the home and then widening our circle of love to encompass our ward members, our less active and nonmember neighbors, and also those who have passed beyond the veil" (Jack H. Goaslind, Jr., "Reach Out to Our Father's Children," *Ensign*, May 1981).

"Charity is not just a precept or a principle, nor is it just a word to describe actions or attitudes. Rather, it is an internal condition that must be developed and experienced in order to be understood" (C. Max Caldwell, "Love of Christ," *Ensign*, Nov. 1992, 29–30).

"When you get the Spirit of God, you feel full of kindness, charity, long-suffering, and you are willing all the day long to accord to every man that which you want yourself" (John Taylor, *Teachings of the Presidents of the Church: John Taylor*, 2011, 20–29).

"We ought to be full of charity, of brotherly kindness and affection and love one towards another and love towards all men. We ought to feel as our Heavenly Father does" (John Taylor, *Teachings of the Presidents of the Church: John Taylor*, 2011, 20–29).

"The more we serve our fellowmen in appropriate ways, the more substance there is to our souls" (Spencer W. Kimball, "President Kimball Speaks Out on Service to Others," *New Era*, March 1981, 47–49).

"Kindness has many synonyms—love, service, charity. But I like the word kindness because it implies action. It seems like something you and I can do. Kindness can be shown in so many ways" (Betty Jo Jepsen, "Kindness—A Part of God's Plan," *Ensign*, Nov. 1990).

GOSPEL ART:

Jesus Christ— (1 KIT, 1 GAB)

Christ Healing the Sick at Bethesda—(42 GAB)

The Good Samaritan—(44 GAB)

Jesus Washing the Apostles' Feet—(22 KIT, 55 GAB)

Jesus Praying in Gethsemane—(227 KIT, 56 GAB)

Jesus Carrying a Lost Lamb—(64 GAB)

King Benjamin Addresses His People—(307 KIT, 74 GAB)

The Foundation of the Relief Society—(98 GAB)

The Sermon on the Mount—(212 KIT, 39 GAB)

Jesus Blesses the Nephite Children—(84 GAB)

Service—(115 GAB)

VIDEOS:

- "Charity Never Faileth," President Thomas S. Monson: http://www.lds.org/media-library/video/general-conference-october-2010?lang=eng&query=character#2010-09-0040-president-thomas-s-monson

- "Charity: An Example of the Believers": http://www.lds.org/ldsorg/v/sp?autoplay=true&index=2&locale=0&sourceId=ab516e2109b6210VgnVCM100000176f620a&vgnextoid=bd163ca6e9aa3210VgnVCM1000003a94610aRCRD

- "Charity: The Pure Love of Christ": http://www.lds.org/pages/general-rs-meeting-sept-2010?lang=eng&query=charity

- "How Do I Love Thee?—Elder Jeffrey R. Holland": www.lds.org/ldsorg/v/index.jsp?vgnextoid=bd163ca6e9aa3210VgnVCM1000003a94610aRCRD&locale=0

OBJECT LESSONS:

- Introduce the sisters to several great websites where they can go with their families to choose service projects in their area where they can reach out to others in their community:
  - www.servenet.org
  - www.volunteermatch.org
  - www.idealist.org
  - www.serve.gov
  - www.volunteers.com
  - www.nationalservice.gov

- Show a set of silverware and ask the sisters to describe their different functions:
  - Fork = stabs the item with an attitude of "This is mine!"
  - Knife = cuts everything to be a different size or separate it
  - Spoon = gathers small things together

  Which kind of service do you want to give? Lord, make me a spoon!

- Teach the sisters how to knit or crochet so that during your lesson they can begin making leper bandages to send to the Church's Humanitarian Center. You'll find tons of things your Relief Society can do to serve at www.ldsphilanthropies.org. Items can be sent to:

  LDS Philanthropies
  15 E. South Temple
  2nd Floor East
  Salt Lake City, UT 84150
  Telephone: (801) 240-5567

- While teaching your lesson, remove your jacket, belt, shoes and unbutton some buttons on your sleeves, without explaining why. At the end say, "You probably won't remember a word I said by the time you get home, but you will never forget what I did. Actions speak louder than words." We can talk about being Christ-like, but when we serve, we truly are Christ-like.

🙠 Pass around a mirror and ask the sisters to look in it. Ask them when they focused on their own image if they were able to see anyone else? (No). By serving others we focus less on our own problems and challenges and gain improved perspective.

🙠 Make "Friendship Fudge" during the lesson by passing around gallon size bags of ingredients that the sisters have to squish together to form the sweet treat. Recipe:
  • 4 cups powdered sugar
  • 3 ounces softened cream cheese
  • ½ cup softened margarine
  • ½ cup cocoa
  • 1 tsp. vanilla
  • ½ cup chopped nuts
  When it is mixed together, roll it into a log and slice and serve.

🙠 Get eight cups that fit into each other. Read 2 Peter 2:5 and label each of your cup layers according to the things Paul talks about, starting with faith and ending with charity at the top. Then read 1 Corinthians 13:4 and label 16 popsicle sticks with each one of the descriptions about charity. Glue a little flower to the top of each popsicle stick, and you now have a cute flower arrangement that shows how we go from faith to charity.

ARTICLES:

🙠 Henry B. Eyring, "Feeding His Lambs," *Liahona*, Feb. 2008.
🙠 Derek A. Cuthbert, "The Spirituality of Service," *Ensign*, May 1990, 12–13.
🙠 Jeffrey R. Holland, " 'Charity Never Faileth': A Discussion on Relief Society" *Liahona*, Mar. 2011.
🙠 V. Dallas Merrell, "A Vision of Service," *Ensign*, Dec. 1996, 10–15.

- Spencer W. Kimball, "Small Acts of Service," *Ensign*, Dec. 1974, 2–7.
- Russell C. Taylor, "The Joy of Service," *Ensign*, Nov. 1984, 23–24.
- Gene R. Cook, "Charity: Perfect and Everlasting Love," *Ensign*, May 2002, 82–83.

CHALLENGE:

Visit the website www.ldscharities.org and select one of the ways you can serve this week. Recruit the help of your family and make a plan to participate in a service project once a month.

SEMINARY SCRIPTURE MASTERY:

2 Nephi 28:7–9   Moses 7:18
Jacob 2:18–19   Leviticus 19:18
Mosiah 2:17   D&C 64:9–11
3 Nephi 11:29   D&C 88:123–24
Moroni 7:45

PREACH MY GOSPEL:

Pages 87, 118, 168–69

"Charity is not just a precept or a principle, nor is it just a word to describe actions or attitudes. Rather, it is an internal condition that must be developed and experienced in order to be understood."

—C. Max Caldwell, "Love of Christ,"
Ensign, Nov. 1992

"Charity is not just a precept or a principle, nor is it just a word to describe actions or attitudes. Rather, it is an internal condition that must be developed and experienced in order to be understood."

—C. Max Caldwell, "Love of Christ,"
Ensign, Nov. 1992

"Charity is not just a precept or a principle, nor is it just a word to describe actions or attitudes. Rather, it is an internal condition that must be developed and experienced in order to be understood."

—C. Max Caldwell, "Love of Christ,"
Ensign, Nov. 1992

"Charity is not just a precept or a principle, nor is it just a word to describe actions or attitudes. Rather, it is an internal condition that must be developed and experienced in order to be understood."

—C. Max Caldwell, "Love of Christ,"
Ensign, Nov. 1992

LESSON TWENTY-ONE

PROCLAIMING THE GOSPEL
TO THE WORLD

Music

"Called to Serve"—*Hymns* #249

"How Will They Know?"—Children's Songbook #271

"I Hope They Call Me on a Mission"—Children's Songbook #169

"I Want to Be a Missionary Now"—Children's Songbook #168

"We'll Bring the World His Truth (Army of Helaman)"—Children's Songbook #172

"What Was Witnessed in the Heavens?—*Hymns* #11

SUMMARY:

There are many people in the world who are pure in heart, who would embrace the fulness of the gospel if they were given the opportunity. We have been given the knowledge of saving ordinances, as well as the divinely commissioned authority to provide them to the nations of the earth.

When we truly feel the Savior's love, we have the natural desire to extend it to those around us. When we do, our joy will be felt for eternity. The Lord entrusts us with this important work and it is our privilege to bring light to a dark world. Our righteous examples can illuminate our neighborhoods and draw the pure in heart to us.

When we help prepare young men and women to serve full-time missions and support them with prayers, food, finances, and referrals while they are laboring in the field, the Lord is pleased with our missionary efforts and we will have an even greater desire to open our mouths and share what we know with a world that is seeking truth and direction. What a thrill it is to be a part of the exciting wave of missionary work happening right now as the Lord hastens His work.

In the spirit of love and kindness, our missionary work is about inviting people, not convincing them, to learn more. Rather than debate doctrine with non-believers, we gently love them and show them the Savior's love. The most important part of effective missionary work is not our carefully chosen words, but the Spirit with which we teach. This is the Lord's work and one of the most important things we can do here on earth.

QUOTES:

"The First Presidency has said that one of the threefold missions of the Church is to proclaim the gospel. If we accept this mission, we should be willing to center our efforts on bringing souls unto the Lord on condition of repentance. In talking of faith and saving souls, you should understand that when the Spirit is present, people are not offended when you share your feelings about the gospel" (M. Russell Ballard, "We Proclaim the Gospel," *Ensign*, Nov. 1986).

"For the Savior's mandate to share the gospel to become part of who we are, we need to make member missionary work a way of life" (Quentin L. Cook, "Be a Missionary All Your Life," *Ensign*, Sept. 2008).

"It is impractical for us to expect that full-time missionaries alone can warn the millions in the world. Members must be finders. If we are in tune, the Spirit of the Lord will speak to us and guide us to those with whom we should share the gospel. The Lord will help us if we will but listen" (Ezra Taft Benson, "President Kimball's Vision of Missionary Work," *Ensign*, July 1985).

"We have long realized that the most important missionary tool is a good member of the Church" (Brian Kelly, "A Visit with Elder Gordon B. Hinckley about Missionary Work," *New Era*, June 1973).

"When we received the special blessing of knowledge of the gospel of Jesus Christ and took upon ourselves the name of Christ by entering the waters of baptism, we also accepted the obligation to share the gospel with others" (L. Tom Perry, "The Past Way of Facing the Future," *Ensign*, Nov. 2009, 75).

"The standard of truth has been erected: no unhallowed hand can stop the work from progressing, persecution may rage, mobs may combine, armies may assemble, calumny may defame, but the truth of God will go forth boldly, nobly, and independent till it has penetrated every continent, visited every clime, swept every country, and sounded in every ear, till the purposes of God shall be accomplished and the great Jehovah shall say the work is done" (Joseph Smith, Church History, *Times and Seasons*, March 1842, 709).

"As Latter-day Saints everywhere, with personal testimonies of these great events, we accept humbly, gratefully, this major responsibility placed upon the Church. We are happy to be engaged in a partnership with our Heavenly Father in the great work of the salvation and exaltation of his children. Willingly we give of our time and our means with which he may bless us to the establishment of his kingdom in the earth. This we know is our first duty and our great opportunity. This spirit has characterized the missionary work of the church of Jesus Christ in all ages. It has been an outstanding mark of the ushering in of the dispensation of the fulness of times--our time. Wherever faithful Latter-day Saints are to be found, this spirit of unselfish sacrifice for the greatest cause in all the earth exists. In a statement published to the world during the last world war, the First Presidency of the Church declared: "No act of ours or of the Church must interfere with this God-given mandate" (Ezra Taft Benson, *Ensign*, Apr. 1942, 91).

"After all that has been said, the greatest and most important duty is to preach the Gospel" (Joseph Smith, *History of the Church*, 2:478, Apr. 1837).

GOSPEL ART:

Esther—(21 GAB)
Boy Jesus in the Temple—(205 KIT, 34 GAB)
John Preaching in the Wilderness—(207 KIT)
Calling of the Fishermen—(209 KIT, 37 GAB)
Go Ye Therefore—(235 KIT, 61 GAB)
Abinadi before King Noah—(308 KIT, 75 GAB)
Alma Baptizes in the Waters of Mormon—(309 KIT, 76 GAB)
Four Missionaries to the Lamanites—(418 KIT)
Missionaries Teach the Gospel of Jesus Christ—(612 KIT)
Missionaries: Elders—(109 GAB)
Missionaries: Sisters—(110 GAB)

VIDEOS:

- "The Heart and a Willing Mind": http://lds.org/library/display /0,4945,6635-1-4786-3,00.html

- "Church Growth by Stake": http://lds.org/library/display/0,4945 ,6635-1-4786-7,00.html

- "Why Mormons Send Missionaries Around the World": http://lds. org/media-library/video/our-faith?lang=eng&start=13&end=24

- "By Small and Simple Things: Sharing the Gospel": http://lds.org/ media-library/video/strength-of-youth-media?lang=eng#2010- 12-05-by-small-and-simple-things-sharing-the-gospel

- "A Mighty Change: Conversion": http://lds.org/media-library /video/strength-of-youth-media?lang=eng&start=13&end=24 #2010-12-14-a-mighty-change-conversion

OBJECT LESSONS:

- The spirit of missionary work will fill your classroom as you invite the sisters to share their conversion stories.

- Invite the sisters to be creative in pairs and take turns doing "door approaches" by knocking on the door to your classroom and presenting a gospel message. You'll be amazed at how innovative they'll be.

- Set up a row of dominoes on the front table and then watch the chain reaction as you knock the first one down. Compare that to all of the lives that are touched for good by just one member of the Church being a good missionary.

- Pass out copies of the Book of Mormon and invite the sisters to write their testimonies inside the flap. Give the copies to your ward missionaries to pass out to their investigators.

- Invite the full-time missionaries to share some conversion stories and experiences with your class.

- Before class, put a bunch of pieces of candy in a bag. Tell the class that we often feel we can't make any difference as just one person. Show one piece of candy and explain that it represents you, a member of the Church. Show another piece of candy, which represents one person you talk to about the gospel. That person then tells someone else about the gospel who tells another person and so on. Add a piece of candy next to each person who talks about the gospel. Talk about how our simple efforts can grow the Church exponentially. Pass around the candy to the class, illustrating that sharing the gospel can be *sweet*!

- Take pictures of all the sisters in the ward to create a Relief Society photo directory. Part of missionary work is fellowshipping with the Saints and getting to know one another better.

- Place a hard rock in a bowl of water and explain that it represents the heart of some people. Use a squirt gun to spray some water on the rock to illustrate how when we try to explain the gospel to hard-hearted people it just rolls off. Show a sponge in the shape of a heart. Use the squirt gun to spray some water on it and point out how the sponge quickly absorbs the water. Some people will soak up the gospel like sponges! Jesus Christ is the Living Water. Not everyone will be ready to accept the gospel, but we still have to offer them the opportunity.

ARTICLES:

- Earl C. Tingey, "Missionary Service," *Ensign*, May 1998, 39–41.
- Thomas S. Monson, "That All May Hear," *Ensign*, May 1995.
- M. Russell Ballard, "Creating a Gospel-Sharing Home," *Ensign*, May 2006.
- Dallin H. Oaks, "Sharing the Gospel," *Ensign*, Nov. 2001.
- Dallin H. Oaks, "The Role of Members in Conversion," *Ensign*, Mar. 2003, 52.
- Ezra Taft Benson, "President Kimball's Vision of Missionary Work," *Ensign*, July 1985.

CHALLENGE:

Invite the full-time missionaries in your area over to have dinner. Ask them about their investigators and find out what you can do to help. Invite them to teach one of their investigators in your home or go with them to teach.

SEMINARY SCRIPTURE MASTERY:

Moroni 10:4–5

Isaiah 29:13–14

Jeremiah 16:16

Romans 1:16

Revelation 14:6–7

Joseph Smith History 1:15–20

D&C 18:10, 15–16

PREACH MY GOSPEL:

Pages 2, 4–5, 10–11, 84, 93, 144–45, 175, 219

"For the Savior's mandate to share the gospel to become part of who we are, we need to make member missionary work a way of life."

—Quentin L. Cook, "Be a Missionary All Your Life," *Ensign*, Sept. 2008

"For the Savior's mandate to share the gospel to become part of who we are, we need to make member missionary work a way of life."

—Quentin L. Cook, "Be a Missionary All Your Life," *Ensign*, Sept. 2008

"For the Savior's mandate to share the gospel to become part of who we are, we need to make member missionary work a way of life."

—Quentin L. Cook, "Be a Missionary All Your Life," *Ensign*, Sept. 2008

"For the Savior's mandate to share the gospel to become part of who we are, we need to make member missionary work a way of life."

—Quentin L. Cook, "Be a Missionary All Your Life," *Ensign*, Sept. 2008

PRAYER—A COMMANDMENT AND A BLESSING

Music

"Before Thee, Lord, I Bow My Head"—*Hymns* #158
"Come Unto Him"—*Hymns* #114
"Did You Think To Pray?"—*Hymns* #140
"Prayer Is The Soul's Sincerest Desire"—*Hymns* #145
"Sweet Hour of Prayer"—*Hymns* #142
"A Child's Prayer"—Children's Songbook #12
"Joseph Smith's First Prayer"—*Hymns* #26

SUMMARY:

Prayer is the vehicle we can use to communicate with our Father in Heaven. We are commanded to pray always unto the Father and only Him. We can pray either vocally or silently, asking for guidance and strength, confessing our sins, showing gratitude, and requesting specific blessings. We should pray individually and as families each day. God answers our prayers by granting us increased ability or by inspiring others to help us. As we pray, we draw closer to our Heavenly Father until His will is the same as ours.

One of the most powerful truths we can know is that the Creator of the universe knows and loves us personally. Prayer enables us to talk to our Father who is in heaven as if He were speaking with us face to face here on earth. How wonderful it is not only that God truly hears our prayers, but that He wants to hear them. Inspired lives includes daily personal prayer, family prayer and, if we are married, companionship prayer. Those prayers should be filled with active listening.

QUOTES:

"Prayer being the soul's sincere desire, uttered or unexpressed, pray for your righteous desires. But never forget that whatever our prayers are, we can supplement our heavenly request with some positive action on our part" (Franklin D. Richards, "The Importance of Prayer," *Ensign*, May 1972).

"Prayer is a supernal gift of our Father in Heaven to every soul. Think of it: the absolute Supreme Being, the most all-knowing, all-seeing, all-powerful personage, encourages you and me, as insignificant as we are, to converse with Him as our Father" (Richard G. Scott, "Using the Supernal Gift of Prayer," *Ensign*, May 2007).

"A key to improved prayer is to learn to ask the right questions. Consider changing from asking for the things you want to honestly seeking what He wants for you. Then as you learn His will, pray that you will be led to have the strength to fulfill it" (Richard G. Scott, "Using the Supernal Gift of Prayer," *Ensign*, May 2007).

"Our Father in Heaven has promised us peace in times of trial and has provided a way for us to come to Him in our need. He has given us the privilege and power of prayer" (Rex D. Pinegar, "Peace through Prayer," *Ensign*, May 1993, 65–68).

"A return to the old pattern of prayer, family prayer in the homes of the people, is one of the basic medications that would check the dread disease that is eroding the character of our society" (Gordon B. Hinckley, "The Blessings of Family Prayer," *Ensign*, Feb. 1991, 2–5).

"Men and women of integrity, character, and purpose have ever recognized a power higher than themselves and have sought through prayer to be guided by such power" (Thomas S. Monson, "The Prayer of Faith," *Ensign*, Aug. 1995).

"I can think of no greater teaching to our children than that of the power of prayer" (L. Tom Perry, "Our Father Which Art in Heaven," *Ensign*, Nov. 1983, 11–13).

GOSPEL ART:

Jesus Praying in Gethsemane—(227 KIT, 56 GAB)
Enos Praying—(305 KIT, 72 GAB)
Moroni Hides the Plates in the Hill Cumorah—(320 KIT, 86 GAB)
The First Vision—(403 KIT, 90 GAB)
Young Boy Praying—(605 KIT, 111 GAB)
Family Prayer—(606 KIT, 112 GAB)
Daniel in the Lions' Den—(117 KIT, 26 GAB)

VIDEOS:

- "And My Soul Hungered": http://lds.org/library/display/0,4945,6635-1-4786-2,00.html

- "How God Talks to Us Today": http://lds.org/media-library/video/our-faith?lang=eng

- "President Monson Talks About Prayer": http://www.lds.org/media-library/video/2011-10-66-president-monson-talks-about-prayer?lang=eng

- "Getting Answers to Prayers": http://www.lds.org/media-library/video/2010-07-014-getting-answers-to-prayers?lang=eng

- "Prayer—Sue": http://www.lds.org/media-library/video/2009-04-101-prayer-sue?lang=eng

OBJECT LESSONS:

ஃ Invite the class to share their experiences of trying to find a moment in their hectic lives for personal prayer. Before the discussion ask a volunteer in private to keep raising her hand while you ignore her. You could even acknowledge her, but tell her you need to say a few more things before she can talk. Finally, when you call her have her tell the class of your plan and explain that sometimes our prayers are like that; we do all of the talking and don't let the Lord participate in the discussion.

ஃ As you walk into the room, talk loudly on your mobile phone as if you are talking to a friend. Talk about your plans for the day, the things you need to do, and then ask for advice. Ask the class to compare your conversation to prayer. Remind them that talking on a cell phone is different from prayer in the following ways:
+ God is never out of range.
+ We never "lose the signal."
+ The battery never runs dead.
+ We never run out of minutes.
+ We don't have to remember God's number. Just talk!

ஃ Show a letter that is addressed to someone, but doesn't have a postage stamp on it and ask the class why the postman won't deliver it. Read Alma 33:11 and ask why the prayer of Zenos was heard? Explain that the postage stamp represents sincerity. Sincerity is the postage that delivers our letter (prayer) to Heavenly Father.

ஃ Show the class a shaker of pepper and explain that the pepper represents temptations. Shake some of the pepper into a dish with water in it. Read Doctrine and Covenants 10:5 and ask the class what we should do when we're tempted? Now show the class a bar of soap and explain that it represents prayer. Invite a volunteer to rub her fingers on the bar of soap and then touch the surface of the water in the dish. (The pepper will move to the sides of the dish.) Brigham Young once said, "Prayer keeps a man from sin, and sin keeps a man from prayer."

Ask the class to take several long, deep breaths. There are interesting breathing exercises you can find online you could have the sisters do for a few minutes. We need to breathe to stay alive. When we breathe, we inhale oxygen and exhale carbon dioxide. Breathing actually cleanses us. Just as breathing can bring cleansing to our physical bodies, so can prayer to our spiritual bodies. Prayer can be a lot like breathing. We need to pray to stay spiritually alive. Paul states in 1 Thessalonians 5:17 that we are to "pray without ceasing." We can't live if our breathing ceases. We need to connect with God in prayer. It is essential to our spiritual health and survival!

ARTICLES:

- David A. Bednar, "Pray Always," *Ensign*, Nov. 2008.
- Dallin H. Oaks, "The Language of Prayer," *Ensign*, May 1993.
- Russell M. Nelson, "Lessons from the Lord's Prayers," *Ensign*, May 2009.
- James E. Faust, "The Lifeline of Prayer," *Ensign*, May 2002.
- N. Eldon Tanner "Importance and Efficacy of Prayer," *Ensign*, Aug. 1971.
- Spencer W. Kimball, "Pray Always," *Ensign*, Oct. 1981.
- Dan B. Skoubye, "Enriching Our Prayers," *Ensign*, Aug. 2002, 53.
- Richard G. Scott, "Recognizing Answers to Prayer," *New Era*, Aug. 2003, 5.

CHALLENGE:

Say a prayer today without asking for anything; just give thanks to the Lord. Offer another prayer tomorrow, focusing on other people's needs and how you could help them. Don't mention any of your needs. (Heavenly Father already knows about them anyway.) Write in your journal about those two conversations with Heavenly Father.

SEMINARY SCRIPTURE MASTERY:

2 Nephi 32:8–9   D&C 10:5

James 1:5–6   D&C 25:12

D&C 8:2–3

PREACH MY GOSPEL:

Pages 39, 73, 93–95

"I can think of no greater teaching to our children than that of the power of prayer."

—L. Tom Perry, "Our Father Which Art in Heaven,"
Ensign, Nov. 1983

"I can think of no greater teaching to our children than that of the power of prayer."

—L. Tom Perry, "Our Father Which Art in Heaven,"
Ensign, Nov. 1983

"I can think of no greater teaching to our children than that of the power of prayer."

—L. Tom Perry, "Our Father Which Art in Heaven,"
Ensign, Nov. 1983

LESSON TWENTY-THREE
INDIVIDUAL RESPONSIBILITY

Music

"Put Your Shoulder to the Wheel"—*Hymns #252*
"Come, Come, Ye Saints"—*Hymns #30*
"Have I Done Any Good?"—*Hymns #223*
"I Have Work Enough to Do"—*Hymns #224*
"Improve the Shining Moments"—*Hymns #226*
"Let Us All Press On"—*Hymns #243*

SUMMARY:

We are commanded to be industrious and anxiously engaged in good works. That's what Heavenly Father does. The Lord has given us free agency and expects us to do all we can for ourselves and others. Work gives us purpose and helps us provide for our wants and needs. Doing our best is a matter of integrity, instilling an attitude of honor in all that we do. Idleness is contrary to the gospel.

As mothers, we need to teach our children to work and not rely on others for everything. In order to learn to accept responsibility, children need to see us work, work beside us, and learn to work alone. The Lord will hold us responsible for what we do with our time and resources.

QUOTES:

"By our very endowment as children of an Eternal Father, we have had implanted within our souls the urgency to be free. It is natural for us to want to be accountable for our own fates, because there is a whispering within us confirming that this accountability is absolutely essential to the attainment of our eternal destiny. . . . If we allow ourselves to accept dependency and regulation and to cease valuing independence and self-accountability, then we are vulnerable to the forces that destroy freedom" (Dean L. Larsen, "Self-Accountability and Human Progress," *Ensign*, May 1980).

"I have found nothing in the battle of life that has been of more value to me than to perform the duty of today to the best of my ability; and I know that where young men do this, they will be better prepared for the labors of tomorrow" (Heber J. Grant, *Teachings of Presidents of the Church: Heber J. Grant*, 2002, 114).

"Let us realize that the privilege to work is a gift, that the power to work is a blessing, that love of work is success" (David O. McKay, *True to the Faith*, comp. Llewelyn R. McKay, Salt Lake City: Bookcraft, 1966, 287).

"I do not believe people can be happy unless they have work to do. If we learn to work early in life we will be better individuals, better members of families, better neighbors, and better disciples of Jesus Christ, who Himself learned to work as a carpenter" (Neal A. Maxwell, "Gospel of Work," *Friend*, June 1975, 7).

"Some of us are too content with what we may already be doing. We stand back in the "eat, drink, and be merry" mode when opportunities for growth and development abound" (James E. Faust, "I Believe I Can, I Knew I Could," *Ensign*, Nov. 2002).

GOSPEL ART:

Ruth Gleaning in the Fields—(17 GAB)
Building the Ark—(102 KIT, 7 GAB)
Calling of the Fishermen—(209 KIT, 37 GAB)
The Good Samaritan—(218 KIT, 44 GAB)

Mary and Martha—(219 KIT, 45 GAB)

Parable of the Ten Virgins—(53 GAB)

Go Ye Therefore—(235 KIT, 61 GAB)

Jesus Carrying a Lost Lamb—(64 GAB)

Jesus at the Door—(237 KIT, 65 GAB)

Enos Praying—(305 KIT, 72 GAB)

Captain Moroni Raises the Title of Liberty—(312 KIT, 79 GAB)

The Brother of Jared Sees the Finger of the Lord—(318 KIT, 85 GAB)

Joseph Smith Seeks Wisdom in the Bible—(402 KIT, 89 GAB)

Joseph Smith Translating the Book of Mormon—(92 GAB)

The Foundation of the Relief Society—(98 GAB)

Handcart Pioneers Approaching the Salt Lake Valley—(414 KIT, 102 GAB)

Service—(115 GAB)

VIDEOS:

- "Willing and Worthy to Serve": http://www.lds.org/media-library/video/2012-04-3060-president-thomas-s-monson?lang=eng

- "The Blessing of Work": www.lds.org/ldsorg/v/index.jsp?locale=0&vgnextoid=22dfd7256ec8b010VgnVCM1000004d82620aRCRD&year=2005

- "The Three Rs of Choice": http://www.lds.org/media-library/video/2010-10-3060-president-thomas-s-monson?lang=eng

- "Doing the Right Thing at the Right Time, without Delay": http://www.lds.org/media-library/video/2011-10-1050-elder-jose-l-alonso?lang=eng

OBJECT LESSONS:

❧ Tell the class, "I want you to follow what I say here. Hold your hands up in front of you. Now, when I say, 'Go,' clap them together. Let's start. One . . . two . . . three" (you clap your hands together). The class will most likely clap their hands together when you do, not when you say "go." Point out to them that they followed what you did, not what you said. Live the gospel. Don't just talk about it.

❧ Hold up the hanger and ask what it is used for. (Hanging up clothes) Ask if anyone can name any other things a hanger can be used for. They might suggest things like opening a locked car door, roasting marshmallows, cleaning a clogged drain or making craft projects. Read Doctrine and Covenants 60:2 and Doctrine and Covenants 82:18. Ask what these scriptures have to do with the hanger. Remind everyone that the Lord expects us to do more than just "hang around." Talk about how we should work at school, the office, at home, as well as actively participate in the Lord's work at church.

❧ Ask a volunteer to make a cake and choose between a wooden spoon or an electric mixer. When we do tasks on our own it usually takes longer, but if we use a greater power (Heavenly Father), it's easier. His power source can help us accomplish our tasks. If your Church building allows you to bake in the kitchen, cook the cake in the oven during class and enjoy it together at the end of class.

❧ Before class, put a $5 bill in someone's scriptures without her noticing. (Choose someone who is a good sport and who won't be leaving during the lesson.) During the lesson, ask the sister to bring her scriptures up to the front of class to help you with something. Ask her "Do you know me as a friend and trust me? Do you think that I would lie to you? If I gave you a very simple task that you could accomplish right up here with me, would you do it?" After she answers, tell her "Give me $5." She will be flustered and won't feel as though she can help you. Reach for her scriptures and take the $5 bill out. Explain that God will never give us a task that he has not already given us the talents and ability to accomplish. We may not see them at first, but he has put them there, and we must ask for his help and strength in doing his will.

ARTICLES:

- ❧ Robert S. Wood, "On the Responsible Self," *Ensign*, Mar. 2002.
- ❧ H. David Burton, "The Blessing of Work," *Ensign*, Dec. 2009.
- ❧ Orson Scott Card, "The Elbow-Grease Factor: How to Teach Your Children to Love Work," *Ensign*, Aug. 1978.
- ❧ Kathleen Slaugh, "More Than Clean Windows: The Unrecognized Value of Housework," *Ensign*, Oct. 1985.
- ❧ Neal A. Maxwell, "Put Your Shoulder to the Wheel," *Ensign*, May 1998.
- ❧ Jorge F. Zeballos, "Attempting the Impossible," *Ensign*, Nov. 2009.

CHALLENGE:

Write a to-do list of some tasks you need to do that you've been putting off. Decide which days this week you'll do them, and then choose a reward for yourself once they're completed.

SEMINARY SCRIPTURE MASTERY:

1 Nephi 3:7	Matthew 6:24
2 Nephi 2:27	John 7:17
2 Nephi 28:7–9	James 2:17–18
Mosiah 4:30	Revelation 20:12–13
Alma 34:32–34	D&C 14:7
Alma 41:10	D&C 58:26–27
Ether 12:6	D&C 82:3
Ether 12:27	D&C 82:10
Moroni 10:4–5	D&C 88:123–24
Abraham 3:22–23	D&C 89:18–21
Exodus 20:3–17	D&C 130:18–19
Malachi 3:8–10	D&C 130:20–21

PREACH MY GOSPEL:

Pages 89–90

"Let us realize that
the privilege to work is
a gift, that the power to
work is a blessing, that
love of work is success."

—David O. McKay, *True to the Faith*, comp. Llewelyn R.
McKay, Salt Lake City: Bookcraft, 1966

"Let us realize that
the privilege to work is
a gift, that the power to
work is a blessing, that
love of work is success."

—David O. McKay, *True to the Faith*, comp. Llewelyn R.
McKay, Salt Lake City: Bookcraft, 1966

THE WORK OF LATTER-DAY SAINT WOMEN: "UNSELFISH DEVOTION TO THIS GLORIOUS CAUSE"

Music

"Let Us All Press On"—*Hymns* #243

"True to the Faith"—*Hymns* #254

"We Are All Enlisted"—*Hymns* #250

"Have I Done Any Good?"—*Hymns* #223

"Improve the Shining Moments"—*Hymns* #226

"Put Your Shoulder to the Wheel"—*Hymns* #252

SUMMARY:

Faithful women have played vital roles in the growth of the Lord's kingdom on earth since the very beginning. Did you know that the Relief Society is the largest women's organization on earth? There is no limit to the good our sisters can do in the world and in the Church.

Whether we serve in the nursery or on the General Relief Society Board, we are valued and invited to partake of His marvelous work and wonder. Combined with the priesthood, Heavenly Father offers every spiritual gift and blessing He has to every valiant woman. The Lord expects women to seek for light and truth, as well as lead others to Him.

We become Christ-like when we do His work. It is an honor to search for the Lord's lost lambs and to feed His sheep, because we know the Shepherd will return! Women have a natural ability to nurture, serve, and care for others . . . just like the Savior.

QUOTES:

"In order to do our part as women under the Lord's plan, we must stand strong and immovable in faith, strong and immovable in family, and strong and immovable in relief." "My dear sisters, our prophet, whom I sustain with all my heart, has said that there is a better way than the way of the world. He has called upon the women of the Church to stand together for righteousness. He has said that if we are united and speak with one voice, our strength will be incalculable" (Julie B. Beck, "What Latter-day Saint Women do Best: Stand Strong and Immovable," *Ensign*, Nov. 2007).

"Much of what we accomplish in the Church is due to the selfless service of women. Whether in the Church or in the home, it is a beautiful thing to see the priesthood and the Relief Society work in perfect harmony. Such a relationship is like a well-tuned orchestra, and the resulting symphony inspires all of us" (Quentin L. Cook, "LDS Women are Incredible!" *Ensign*, May 2011).

"More than ever we need women of faith, virtue, vision, and charity who can hear and who will respond to the voice of the Lord" (M. Russell Ballard, "Women of Righteousness," BYU Devotional, March 2001, online).

"There is no other arrangement that meets the divine purposes of the Almighty. Man and woman are His creations. Their duality is His design. Their complementary relationships and functions are fundamental to His purposes. One is incomplete without the other" (Gordon B. Hinckley, "The Women in Our Lives," *Ensign*, Nov. 2004).

"What a different world and Church this would be if every Latter-day Saint sister excelled at making, renewing, and keeping covenants; if every sister qualified for a temple recommend and worshipped more often in temples; if every sister studied the scriptures and doctrines of

Christ and knew them so well that she could teach and defend those doctrines at any time or place" (Julie B. Beck, "What Latter-day Saint Women do Best: Stand Strong and Immovable," *Ensign*, Nov. 2007).

GOSPEL ART:

Adam and Eve—(101 KIT, 4 GAB)
Woman at the Well—(217 KIT)
Mary and Martha—(219 KIT, 45 GAB)
Mary and the Resurrected Lord—(233 KIT, 59 GAB)
Go Ye Therefore—(61 GAB)
Jesus Carrying a Lost Lamb—(64 GAB)
Jesus at the Door—(65 GAB)
Emma Smith—(450 KIT, 88 GAB)
Mary Fielding and Joseph F. Smith Crossing the Plains—(412 KIT, 101 GAB)
The Foundation of the Relief Society—(98 GAB)
Missionaries: Sisters—(110 GAB)
Service—(115 GAB)

VIDEOS:

- "Daughters of God": http://www.lds.org/media-library/video/2012-01-015-daughters-of-god?lang=eng

- "Daughters of My Kingdom: The History and Work of Relief Society": http://www.lds.org/media-library/video/2010-09-0010-julie-b-beck?lang=eng

- "Relief Society—Daughters of My Kingdom": http://www.lds.org/media-library/video/2011-09-0020-relief-society-daughters-in-my-kingdom?lang=eng

- "Guardians of Virtue: Young Women Song": http://www.lds.org/media-library/video/2010-12-15-guardians-of-virtue-young-women-song?lang=eng

- "Mothers and Daughters": http://www.lds.org/media-library/video/2010-06-0070-mothers-and-daughters?lang=eng

- "What Manner of Men and Women Ought Ye To Be?": http://www.lds.org/media-library/video/2008-11-05-what-manner-of-men-and-women-ought-ye-to-be?lang=eng

OBJECT LESSONS:

- This might be a fun lesson to invite the Young Women to join the Relief Society. Let them see each other recite the Young Women Values and Relief Society themes. Have the sisters sit according to their generations (under 20, 30–40, 40–50, 60 plus) and have each group answer various questions according to how their age group sees the world.

- Turn off all the lights and cell phones. Open the door a crack and talk about how light enters the room. Have the sisters turn on flashlights or cell phones one at a time, representing the good acts of kindness, service, and leadership we perform. As we bring truth and light to a dark world, it becomes brighter. All of the sisters united in Relief Society can illuminate the world.

- Explain that a few sisters are going to "receive" a calling. Give them each a slip of paper that has a calling written on it. Ask them to line up behind a tape line and behind one another, in order of the importance of their calling. After they are lined up in what they believe is the right order, take each person and lead them to a spot on the tape line, side by side with each other. Talk about how all of the callings are equally important, and that it is the way in which we serve that is important.

ARTICLES:

- Quentin L. Cook, "LDS Women are Incredible!" *Ensign*, May 2011.
- Barbara B. Smith, "Women for the Latter Day," *Ensign*, Nov. 1979.
- Silvia H. Allred, "Every Women Needs Relief Society," *Ensign*, Nov. 2009.
- Julie B. Beck, "Fulfilling the Purpose of Relief Society," *Ensign*, Nov. 2008.
- Henry B. Eyring, "The Enduring Legacy of Relief Society," *Ensign*, Nov. 2009.
- Julie B. Beck, "The Vision of Prophets regarding Relief Society: Faith, Family, Relief," *Ensign*, May 2012.
- Thomas S. Monson, "The Mighty Strength of the Relief Society," *Ensign*, Nov. 1997.

CHALLENGE:

Make an extra effort with the sisters you Visit Teach this month, whether it be an extra phone call, email, text, or home visit. Write a list of all the ways you can truly lift their burdens, give comfort, teach, enrich, and make them feel Christ's love for them.

SEMINARY SCRIPTURE MASTERY:

1 Nephi 3:7	Moses 1:39
Alma 37:6–7	Isaiah 29:13–14
Moroni 7:45	Jeremiah 16:16
Moroni 10:4–5	Daniel 2:44–45

Matthew 5:14–16
Romans 1:16
Ephesians 4:11–14
2 Thessalonians 2:1–3
Revelation 14:6–7

Joseph Smith History 1:15–20
D&C 18:10, 15–16
D&C 58:26–27
D&C 64:23
D&C 137:7–10

PREACH MY GOSPEL:

Pages 84, 87, 118

"There is no other arrangement that meets the divine purposes of the Almighty. Man and woman are His creations. Their duality is His design. Their complementary relationships and functions are fundamental to His purposes. One is incomplete without the other."

—Gordon B. Hinckley, "The Women in Our Lives," *Ensign*, Nov. 2004

"There is no other arrangement that meets the divine purposes of the Almighty. Man and woman are His creations. Their duality is His design. Their complementary relationships and functions are fundamental to His purposes. One is incomplete without the other."

—Gordon B. Hinckley, "The Women in Our Lives," *Ensign*, Nov. 2004

"There is no other arrangement that meets the divine purposes of the Almighty. Man and woman are His creations. Their duality is His design. Their complementary relationships and functions are fundamental to His purposes. One is incomplete without the other."

—Gordon B. Hinckley, "The Women in Our Lives," *Ensign*, Nov. 2004

"There is no other arrangement that meets the divine purposes of the Almighty. Man and woman are His creations. Their duality is His design. Their complementary relationships and functions are fundamental to His purposes. One is incomplete without the other."

—Gordon B. Hinckley, "The Women in Our Lives," *Ensign*, Nov. 2004

THE BIRTH OF JESUS CHRIST: "GOOD TIDINGS OF GREAT JOY"

Music

"I Believe In Christ"—*Hymns* #134
"God Loved Us So He Sent His Son"—*Hymns* #187
"Jesus, Once of Humble Birth"—*Hymns* #196
Christmas Carols—*Hymns* #201–215

SUMMARY:

The account of the Savior's humble birth can powerfully stir our souls. The gospel of Jesus Christ isn't good news . . . it's GREAT news! Jesus Christ's atoning sacrifice is the only way we can return to live with our Heavenly Father. He was born a poor infant under humble circumstances, but He is the creator of this earth and will reign as its king in glory upon His return. By following Jesus Christ, we can find joy in this life and in the next.

While on earth, the Savior organized His church, showed us how to live, and saved us from physical and spiritual death by His redeeming Atonement. Jesus Christ was not just a good man, effective teacher, or inspiring leader; He was the redeemer of the world! As members of the Church, we not only believe that the Savior lived on this earth and died for our sins, but that He still lives. Our lives should reflect those beliefs. Our understanding of the divine mission of Jesus Christ should compel us to action, to show greater love and kindness, and to share His gospel with others.

We should live our lives so that there will be absolutely no question that Mormons are Christians.

QUOTES:

"This little child, born in a stable and cradled in a manger, was a gift from our loving Heavenly Father. He was the promised Redeemer of the world, the Savior of mankind, the Son of the living God. He was with His Father before He came to earth in mortality, the Creator of the earth upon which we stand" (Henry B. Eyring, "The Gift of a Savior," *First Presidency Christmas Devotional*, 2010, online).

"We celebrate the birth of the Son of God, the Creator, our Messiah. We rejoice that the King of kings came to earth, was born in a manger, and lived a perfect life. When Jesus was born, the joy in heaven was so great it could not be contained, and angelic hosts parted the veil, proclaiming unto shepherds 'good tidings of great joy, . . . praising God, and saying, Glory to God in the highest, and on earth peace, good will toward men' " (Dieter F. Uchtdorf, "Seeing Christmas through New Eyes," *First Presidency Christmas Devotional*, 2010, online).

"The Savior's birth, ministry, atoning sacrifice, Resurrection, and promised coming all bear witness to His divinity" (Ezra Taft Benson, "Five Marks of the Divinity of Jesus Christ," *Ensign*, Dec. 2001, 8–15).

"He who is our Great Redeemer was fully qualified to become such, because He was and is the Great Emulator! We, in turn, have been asked to emulate Him" (Neal A. Maxwell, "Jesus, the Perfect Mentor," *Ensign*, Feb. 2001, 8–17).

GOSPEL ART:

Isaiah Writes of Christ's Birth—(113 KIT, 22 GAB)
The Nativity—(201 KIT, 30 GAB)
Boy Jesus in the Temple—(205 KIT, 34 GAB)
John the Baptist Baptizing Jesus—(208 KIT, 35 GAB)

Sermon on the Mount—(212 KIT, 39 GAB)

Triumphal Entry—(223 KIT, 50 GAB)

Jesus Washing the Apostles' Feet—(226 KIT, 55 GAB)

Jesus Praying in Gethsemane—(227 KIT, 56 GAB)

The Betrayal of Jesus—(228 KIT)

The Crucifixion—(230 KIT, 57 GAB)

Jesus' Tomb—(232 KIT, 58 GAB)

Mary and the Resurrected Lord—(233 KIT, 59 GAB)

Jesus Shows His Wounds—(234 KIT, 60 GAB)

The Ascension of Jesus—(236 KIT, 62 GAB)

Jesus at the Door—(237 KIT, 65 GAB)

The Second Coming—(238 KIT, 66 GAB)

The Resurrected Jesus Christ—(239 KIT, 59 GAB)

Jesus Christ Appears to the Nephites—(315 KIT)

Jesus Blesses the Nephite Children—(322 KIT, 84 GAB)

Christ with the Three Nephite Disciples—(324 KIT)

Christ and Children From Around the World—(608 KIT, 116 GAB)

VIDEOS:

- "A Light Unto All: A Christmas Gift": http://mormon.org/video s?gclid=CNjCl9fnsasCFZBb7AodCm04iA

- "Wise Men Still Seek Him": http://www.lds.org/media-library/ video/2011-12-019-wise-men-still-seek-him?lang=eng

- "A Gift to the World": http://www.lds.org/media-library/video /2011-10-001-a-gift-to-the-world?lang=eng

- "Of Curtains, Contentment, and Christmas": http://www.lds.org /media-library/video/2011-12-0010-president-dieter-f-uchtdorf ?lang=eng

- "To This End Was I Born": http://lds.org/media-library/video/ new-testament-presentations?lang=eng

❧   See some of the great testimonies of Christ on www.mormon channel.org/video under "I'm a Mormon," "Bible Videos," and "New Testament Stories."

OBJECT LESSONS:

❧   Give everyone a bottle of water and ask them to talk about how Jesus Christ is like living water.

❧   Give a volunteer a compass and have her show the class where north is. Now turn her in a circle and point her in a different direction, asking her again to tell the class where north is. Jesus is like a compass—wherever we are He can point us in the right direction.

❧   Pass out pictures of Jesus Christ and His life, and ask class members to share what they know about the picture they're holding. This simple exercise becomes an instant testimony meeting as the sisters share how they feel about the Savior and the events of His life.

❧   Invite the sisters to write Christmas cards to your ward missionaries or those serving in the military from your ward.

❧   Ask someone to draw a picture of a horse or temple or something complicated. Now give them a pattern to trace to draw the same thing. Jesus is our pattern to show us how to create our lives here on earth so that we can live an eternal life with Father in heaven.

❧   See more ideas from chapters 2 and 26.

ARTICLES:

- Boyd K. Packer, "Who is Jesus Christ?" *Ensign*, Mar. 2008.
- Gilbert W. Scharffs, "Unique Insights on Christ From the Book of Mormon," *Ensign*, Dec. 1988.
- David B. Haight, "Jesus of Nazareth," *Ensign*, May 1994.
- Monte S. Nyman, "I Am Jesus Christ the Son of God," *Ensign*, Dec. 1999.
- Keith H. Pryor, "The Greatest Story Ever Foretold," *Ensign*, Dec. 1991.
- Ezra Taft Benson, "Five Marks of the Divinity of Jesus Christ," *Ensign*, Dec. 2001.
- Ezra Taft Benson, "Jesus Christ: Our Savior and Redeemer," *Ensign*, June 1990.
- Russell M. Nelson, "Jesus the Christ: Our Master and More," *Ensign*, Apr. 2000.

CHALLENGE:

Decide to make this Christmas one that is entirely focused on the Savior. Rethink your gift choices and the activities you have planned to celebrate this holiday season. Design an advent event calendar that will help you reflect on the Savior each day, such as doing acts of service, studying certain scripture passages, or doing temple work.

SEMINARY SCRIPTURE MASTERY:

Helaman 5:12	Acts 7:55–56
Isaiah 53:3–5	1 Corinthians 15:20–22
John 3:5	D&C 19:16–19
John 17:3	D&C 76:22–24

PREACH MY GOSPEL:

Pages 34, 37, 47–48, 51–52, 60–61

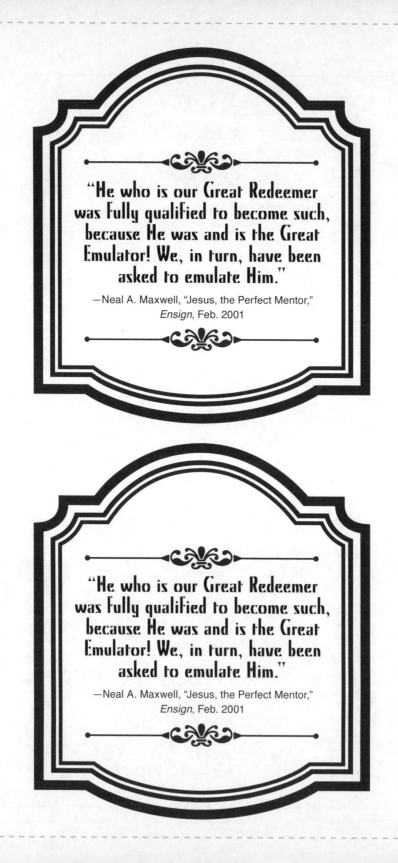

"He who is our Great Redeemer was fully qualified to become such, because He was and is the Great Emulator! We, in turn, have been asked to emulate Him."

—Neal A. Maxwell, "Jesus, the Perfect Mentor," *Ensign*, Feb. 2001

"He who is our Great Redeemer was fully qualified to become such, because He was and is the Great Emulator! We, in turn, have been asked to emulate Him."

—Neal A. Maxwell, "Jesus, the Perfect Mentor," *Ensign*, Feb. 2001

PREPARING FOR THE COMING OF OUR LORD

Music

"I Saw a Mighty Angel Fly"—*Hymns* #15
"Let Zion in Her Beauty Rise"—*Hymns* #41
"Lo, the Mighty God Appearing!"—*Hymns* #55
"Rejoice, Ye Saints of Latter Days"—*Hymns* #290
"The Happy Day at Last Has Come"—*Hymns* #32

SUMMARY:

Before Jesus Christ ascended into heaven, He promised that He would return and counseled us to watch for the signs He would send to help us know when that time would come. Some of the terrifying signs include natural calamities, great wickedness, war, suffering, disease, and famines. As awful as that sounds, there are some very good signs too, which include the Restoration of the Gospel, the coming forth of the Book of Mormon, the gathering of the House of Israel, building the New Jerusalem, Elijah's prophesied return, and temples dotting the earth.

No one knows the hour and day of Christ's return, but as we watch the signs and prepare, we should feel peace and excitement, not fear. The righteous will not be destroyed, but will have the privilege of preparing the earth for His Second Coming. The best way to prepare for the Second Coming of Jesus Christ is to be worthy of the constant companionship of the Holy Ghost, so that we can hear the Spirit's promptings and follow them.

The members of the Church are expected to help gather the House of Israel and stand for truth and righteousness in the latter-days. The Savior's return will actually consist of several phases and assignments:

- He will appear to His people in the temple.
- He will appear with the heads of each dispensation at Adam-ondi-Ahman.
- He will rescue Israel.
- He will cleanse the earth.
- He will judge His people.
- He will usher in the Millennium.
- He will complete the First Resurrection.
- He will rule as King of heaven and earth.

QUOTES:

"There is an urgency in his work. Time is getting short. This sense of urgency in promoting the Lord's kingdom in these last days does not arise out of panic, but out of a desire to move swiftly and surely to establish and strengthen his kingdom among all people who are seeking the light and truth of the gospel, which is God's plan of life for all his children" (Delbert L. Stapley, "To Make a People Prepared for the Lord," *Ensign*, Nov. 1975).

"While we are powerless to alter the fact of the Second Coming and unable to know its exact time, we can accelerate our own preparation and try to influence the preparation of those around us" (Dallin H. Oaks, "Preparation for the Second Coming," *Ensign*, May 2004).

"The Savior's birth, ministry, atoning sacrifice, Resurrection, and promised coming all bear witness to His divinity" (Ezra Taft Benson, "Five Marks of the Divinity of Jesus Christ," *Ensign*, Dec. 2001, 8–15).

"Biblical and modern prophecies give many signs of the Second Coming. These signs of the Second Coming are all around us and seem to be increasing in frequency and intensity" (Dallin H. Oaks, "Preparation for the Second Coming," *Ensign*, May 2004).

"If we are prepared, and if we are trying to draw closer to the Savior every day, we need not fear the events of the Second Coming" (Spencer V. Jones, "Messages from the Doctrine and Covenants: Finding Hope in the Second Coming," *Ensign*, June 2005, 58–60).

"We can't look forward to the Second Coming of the Savior without there being a restitution of all things, and that's the message of The Church of Jesus Christ of Latter-day Saints" (LeGrand Richards, "The Second Coming of Christ," *Ensign*, May 1978, 74–76).

"Before the second coming of Jesus Christ, certain promised signs and wonders are to take place, making it possible for his Saints to know the approximate time of his coming" (Bernard P. Brockbank, "The Leaves are Commencing to Show on the Fig Tree," *Ensign*, May 1976, 74–75).

"We need to make both temporal and spiritual preparation for the events prophesied at the time of the Second Coming" (Dallin H. Oaks, "Preparation for the Second Coming," *Ensign*, May 2004, 7–10).

"We know the prophecies of the future. We know the final outcome. We know the world collectively will not repent, and, consequently, the last days will be filled with much pain and suffering. Therefore, we could throw up our hands and do nothing but pray for the end to come so the millennial reign could begin. To do so would forfeit our right to participate in the grand event we are all awaiting. We must all become players in the winding-up scene, not spectators. We must do all we can to prevent calamities and then do everything possible to assist and comfort the victims of tragedies that do occur" (Glenn L. Pace, "A Thousand Times," *Ensign*, Nov. 1990).

"We surely have been warned and forewarned about our time, a period in which the compression of challenges may make a year seem like a decade. Members will be cleverly mocked and scorned by those in the "great and spacious building," representing the pride of the world. No matter, for ere long, He who was raised on the third day will raze that spacious but third-class hotel!" (Neal A. Maxwell, "Overcome . . . Even As I Also Overcame," *Ensign*, May 1987)

GOSPEL ART:

Mary and the Resurrected Lord—(233 KIT, 59 GAB)
Jesus Shows His Wounds—(234 KIT, GAB 60)
Go Ye Therefore—(235 KIT, 61 GAB)
The Ascension of Jesus—(236 KIT, 62 GAB)
Jesus at the Door—(237 KIT, 65 GAB)
The Second Coming—(238 KIT, 66 GAB)
The Resurrected Jesus Christ—(239 KIT)
Jesus Appears to the Nephites—(315 KIT)
Jesus Teaching in the Western Hemisphere—(316 KIT, 82 GAB)
Jesus Blesses the Nephite Children—(322 KIT, 84 GAB)
Christ Asks for the Records—(323 KIT)
Christ with the Three Nephite Disciples—(324 KIT)
The Bible and Book of Mormon: Two Witnesses—(326 KIT)
Christ and Children from around the World—(608 KIT, 116 GAB)
Missionaries Teach the Gospel of Jesus Christ—(612 KIT)
The First Vision—(403 KIT, 90 GAB)

VIDEOS:

- There is a three part video series called "The Second Coming": http://www.lds.org/media-library/video/2012-06-2480-the-second-coming-segment-1?lang=eng

- "Preparing for the Second Coming": http://www.lds.org/media-library/video/2010-07-039-preparing-for-the-second-coming?lang=eng

- "Be Not Troubled": http://www.lds.org/media-library/video

/2010-07-038-be-not-troubled?lang=eng

- "They That Are Wise": http://www.lds.org/media-library/video /2010-07-14-they-that-are-wise?lang=eng

- "Terror, Triumph, and a Wedding Feast": http://www.lds.org /media-library/video/2004-09-04-terror-triumph-and-a-wedding -feast?lang=eng

- "Watchmen on the Tower": http://www.lds.org/media-library/ video/2010-07-23-watchmen-on-the-tower?lang=eng

OBJECT LESSONS:

- Invite a volunteer to build a structure with building blocks on her lap. Ask the sisters sitting next to her to jiggle her shoulders or legs. Her structure will most likely fall. Now ask her to build one on top of a table at the front of the room. Invite some sisters to try to jiggle her again. This time, her structure won't fall because it has the stability of the table. Our testimonies need to be built on the Atonement of the Savior. That is the solid foundation that will prevent our testimonies and lives from falling apart. The kingdom of God has been restored to the earth again and we are a part of its growth and we build Christ-like lives.

- Ask for two volunteers to "draw the lesson" in front of the class as you study the scriptures together and talk about the Second Coming. Help them to truly visualize themselves playing a role in His return.

- Have ten sisters act out the parable of the Wise and Foolish virgins and identify how they can be better prepared for the Savior's arrival.

- Draw a timeline that lists the signs that need to be fulfilled before

Christ's return, as well as the things that He will do when He comes again. Talk about the spiritual and physical preparedness we will need to have to be a part of each phase.

ঌ See more ideas from chapters 2 and 25.

ARTICLES:

ঌ M. Russell Ballard, "When Shall These Things Be?" *Ensign*, Dec. 1996, 56–61.

ঌ Dallin H. Oaks, "Preparation for the Second Coming," *Ensign*, May 2004, 7–10.

ঌ Delbert L. Stapley, "To Make A People Prepared for the Lord," *Ensign*, Nov. 1975, 47–49.

ঌ Bernard P. Brockbank, "The Leaves Are Commencing To Show on the Fig Tree," *Ensign*, May 1976, 74–75.

ঌ LeGrand Richards, "The Second Coming of Christ," *Ensign*, May 1978, 74–76.

ঌ Spencer V. Jones, "Finding Hope in the Second Coming," *Ensign*, June 2005, 58–60.

ঌ Dallin H. Oaks, "Preparation for the Second Coming," *Ensign*, May 2004.

ঌ Lynn G. Robbins, "Oil in Our Lamps," *Ensign*, June 2007.

CHALLENGE:

Make a list of the things you need to do this week to prepare temporally and spiritually for the Savior's Second Coming. For example, do you have food storage and a tent? Can you recognize the Lord when He speaks to you?

SEMINARY SCRIPTURE MASTERY:

Moses 7:18
Exodus 20:3–17
Job 19:25–26
Luke 24:36–39
John 14:15

2 Timothy 3:1–5
Revelation 20:12–13
D&C 14:7
D&C 64:23
D&C 130:18–19

PREACH MY GOSPEL:

Pages 37, 47–48, 51–52, 59–61

"The Savior's birth, ministry, atoning sacrifice, Resurrection, and promised coming all bear witness to His divinity."

—Ezra Taft Benson, "Five Marks of the Divinity of Jesus Christ," *Ensign*, Dec. 2001

"The Savior's birth, ministry, atoning sacrifice, Resurrection, and promised coming all bear witness to His divinity."

—Ezra Taft Benson, "Five Marks of the Divinity of Jesus Christ," *Ensign*, Dec. 2001

WEBSITE RESOURCES

No need to reinvent the wheel, especially when you're using that wheel to drive on the Information Super Highway! The Internet has an endless resource of ideas, recipes, downloads, crafts, lesson material, music, and instructions for almost anything you'd like to do in your Relief Society Sunday lessons.

Allow me to give you a serious word of caution about doing on-line searches. If you enter "Women" into a search engine you will get suggestions for links to all kinds of horrible pornographic websites. You must type in "LDS Women" or "Relief Society," and even then, look at the description of the site before you click on it!

LDS WEBSITE RESOURCES:

- www.lds.org—The official website of the Church of Jesus Christ of Latter-day Saints. This should be your first stop on the Web.
- www.jennysmith.net
- www.theideadoor.com/
- www.mormons.org
- www.angelfire.com
- http://www.mormonfind.com
- www.lightplanet.com/mormons
- www.ldsworld.com/
- www.ldsteach.com
- www.JeanniGould.com
- www.mormontown.org
- www.sugardoodle.net
- www.ldssplash.com
- www.ldstoday.com

MERCHANDISE:

- www.ldscatalog.com—Church distribution center to order materials
- www.byubookstore.com
- www.ldsliving.com
- www.deseretbook.com
- www.ctr-ring.com

RELIEF SOCIETY BLOGS:

- http://enrichmentideas.blogspot.com/
- http://thereliefsocietyblog.blogspot.com/
- www.hollyscorner.com/blog/lds-resources/relief-society/
- www.mormonmomma.com/index.php/category/church/relief-society/
- http://lds.families.com/blog/category/1071
- http://segullah.org/daily-special/putting-the-relief-in-relief-society/
- http://feastupontheordblog.org/2009/07/27/coming-up-in-relief-society-and-melchizedek-priesthood-for-2010-and-2011/
- http://happyjellybeans.blogspot.com

INTERNET GROUPS:

I highly recommend that you join a Yahoo Group. It's free to join and you'll meet some of the nicest people around! People share helpful ideas and tips in a real-time setting. You can receive the emails individually or as a daily digest. Some groups are more active than others so the quantity of emails will vary. No reason to reinvent the wheel when another great Relief Society teacher has already done it out there somewhere!

- http://groups.yahoo.com/group/ReliefSociety-L/
- http://uk.groups.yahoo.com/group/Relief_SocietyLDS/
- http://groups.yahoo.com/group/ldsreliefsocietypresidency/
- http://groups.yahoo.com/group/LDSReliefSocietyMeetings/

CLIP ART:

I'm thankful for talented artists who share their wonderful creations with me, since I have trouble drawing decent stick people! Here are some of those generous artists:

Most of the websites mentioned above, plus the following:

- www.christysclipart.com
- http://www.graphicgarden.com/
- http://designca.com/lds/
- www.coloringbookfun.com
- www.stums.org/closet/html/index.html
- http://www.oneil.com.au/lds/pictures.html
- http://lds.about.com/library/gallery/clipart/blclipart_gallery_ subindex.htm
- www.free-clip-art.net
- www.coloring.ws/coloring.html
- www.apples4theteacher.com

MUSIC:

- www.lds.org/music
- www.mormonchannel.org
- https://www.lds.org/youth/music
- www.ldsmusicians.com
- www.yldsr.com
- www.defordmusic.com
- www.Radio.ldsmusicnow.com

- http://lds.about.com/library/clipart/blnewera_music_1975. htm
- (Great index of all sheet music offered in the New Era and Ensign magazines from 1975–1989.)
- www.ldsmusicworld.com
- www.ldsmusictoday.com
- www.ldsmusicsource.com
- www.ldspianosolo.com
- www.deseretbook.com/LDS-Music/Sheet-Music-Downloads /s/1395

ABOUT THE AUTHOR

Trina Boice grew up in California and currently lives in Las Vegas. In 2004 she was honored as the California Young Mother of the Year, an award that completely amuses her four sons. She earned two bachelor's degrees from BYU where she competed on the speech and debate team and the ballroom dance team. She was president of the National Honor Society Phi Eta Sigma and served as ASBYU Secretary of Student Community Services.

Trina also studied at the University of Salamanca in Spain and later returned there to serve an LDS mission in Madrid for 1½ years. She has a real estate license, travel agent license, two master's degrees, and a black belt in Tae Kwon Do, although she's the first one to admit she'd pass out from fright if she were ever really attacked by a bad guy.

She worked as a legislative assistant for a congressman in Washington D.C. and was given the "Points of Light" award and Presidential Volunteer Service Award for her domestic and international community service. She wrote a column called "The Boice Box" for a newspaper in Georgia, where she lived for fifteen years. She taught Spanish at a private high school and ran an appraisal business with her husband for twenty years. She currently writes for several newspapers and websites.

Trina was selected by KPBS in San Diego to be a political correspondent during the last presidential election. If she told you what she really did she'd have to kill you.

A popular and entertaining speaker, Trina is the author of seventeen books with another one hitting stores soon! You can read more about her books and upcoming events at www.trinaboice.com. She currently teaches online for BYU–I and Le Cordon Bleu Cooking School.

Check out her movie reviews at www.MovieReviewMaven.blogspot.com and author blog at www.BoiceBox.blogspot.com.